PONTIAC
SHOW CARS
EXPERIMENTALS
& SPECIAL EDITIONS!

by Dale Sass

BOOKMAN PUBLISHING
Baltimore, Maryland

Printed in the U.S.A.
Copyright 1986 in U.S.A. by Bookman Dan! Inc.

ISBN 0-934780-83-8

First Printing
First Edition

All rights reserved. No part of this publication may be
reproduced or transmitted in any form or by any means,
electronic or mechanical, including photography or
recording or any information storage or retrieval system
without permission in writing from the publisher.

Inquiries may be directed to:
Bookman Publishing Division
Bookman Dan! Inc.
P.O. Box 13492
Baltimore, Maryland 21203

Contents

Preface..4

Show Cars, Experimentals
and Special Editions................................5

...And Others... 95

Preface

This is a special book for Pontiac enthusiasts, a segment of the population that seems to be growing at a rapid rate. In the past 10 to 15 years, the interest in older Pontiacs has figuratively mushroomed. There was a time, not that long ago, that the only General Motors Division of less interest to auto enthusiasts than Pontiac was Frigidaire. That has all changed with the graceful aging of Pontiac's youth-oriented cars, particularly from the halcyon days of the sixties.

Pontiac's cars and image were turned around completely in the late fifties under the direction of Semon E. Knudsen. His famous quote, "You can sell a young man's car to old people, but you can't sell an old man's car to young people", was taken to heart at Pontiac. Even the pre-Knudsen Silver Streak Pontiacs were good cars, if not as youthful as subsequent Pontiacs. They were the "Fine Cars of the Low Priced Field" as the slogan went, and "Dollar for Dollar You Couldn't Beat A Pontiac". A recent conversation with my father had him recalling my grandfather's 1939 Pontiac DeLuxe Eight and the 1940 Buick Special he traded the Pontiac for. My dad's comment was, "The Pontiac was more car". This was amazing to me in light of the enormous prestige pre-war Buicks enjoy. An enormous amount of respect for past Pontiacs has been generated in recent years. The Pontiac section in "Hemmings Motor News" is now almost as big as Packard's, but, what is most encouraging, is that it is 1959 all over again for Pontiac today. Pontiac is currently "Building Excitement" like no one else in the industry. They seem braced to enjoy another golden era, much like the sixties.

This book is an attempt to place under one cover all of the Pontiac show cars, experimentals and special editions--the cream of the crop of all Pontiacs. Who said a car had to have a flying lady or a prancing horse on it to be drooled over? The cars in this book are the one-off customs and the special editions built in limited numbers. They are not the Catalina sedans and LeMans coupes you see every day. There are probably Pontiacs in this book you never knew existed and we have attempted to include as many of the factory customs as possible. Outside conversions are not covered unless expressly sponsored by the factory, or at least a group of dealers. Those outside conversions would probably fill another book. Although we have tried to cover all of these cars as defined, there have undoubtedly been some left out. For example, all logic tells me there must have been a specially trimmed Bonneville convertible for the 1961 show circuit. I have found specially trimmed Bonneville convertibles for every year from 1958 through 1964, except 1961. I've discovered X-400 convertibles for all years from 1959 through 1964, except 1961. This lapse is all the more amazing as it was the last year of the GM Motoramas for which so many customs were built.

The cars included in this book cover a wide spectrum. The show cars were designed for display at the GM Motoramas or auto shows. Some were specially designed to show interior workings of cars by dissecting them or using clear plastic exterior panels. Other show cars were specially trimmed production cars designed to glamorize those sold to the public. The third group was the unique designs to test public response to new ideas. These were the most exciting as they bore no resemblance to production cars. Experimental cars weren't always shown to the public as they were in-house design studies testing the feasibility of new products. The special editions, unlike other cars in this book, were sold to the public and usually commemorated a specific event. A few of the special editions in this book were not factory-prepared as some were done by dealer organizations for regional promotion. Others were done by outside companies with some degree of factory approval.

This is more than historical perspective. It is a living, growing breed. Only last month, Pontiac surprised everyone with the Trans Sport, a totally fresh design, very much in the same league as the Club de Mer or the Banshee. With Pontiac's successful program of "Building Excitement", there are undoubtedly more exciting cars to come.

Thanks are in order to a number of organizations and individuals without whose help this book would not have been possible. Obviously, Pontiac Motor Division deserves a hearty round of applause for building the cars in the first place. Deserving particular commendation at PMD is John Sawruk, currently head of Pontiac Motorsports and, unofficially, Pontiac's resident historian. He is the one who unearthed the 1959 X-400 photograph, among other things. He has also been instrumental in developing Pontiac's Historical Vehicle Collection so that more of these cars will be saved from the crusher. The staff at Bookman Publishing cannot be overly praised for their help in putting this book together. Of particular note are Tom Bonsall, Ed Lehwald and Liddie Stein. Tom wrote the definitive Pontiac history, "Pontiac: The Complete History 1926-1986". He has guided me through this project from the beginning. Ed wrote the show cars chapter in "Pontiac: The Complete History" and graciously allowed me to expand upon his area of expertise. Finally, I would like to thank Liddie for her artistic prowess in putting this all together in such a handsome fashion.

Long Beach, California
February, 1986

Show Cars, Experimentals and Special Editions

1939 Transparent Deluxe Sedan

Pontiac built its first show car for the General Motors Exhibit at the 1939 New York World's Fair. It was a Deluxe (B-body) sedan with a transparent, Plexiglas plastic body. It was one of the earliest and most dramatic uses of that type of material and was nearly as important for that as it was as a Pontiac show car. Special lighting was used around the car to give the viewing public the effect of seeing it through an x-ray machine. This was a novel idea as prior to 1939 it was a common industry practice to use a chassis without the attached body to display mechanical features. Pontiac's transparent car allowed a presentation of the mechanical aspects of the car in conjunction with the exterior shape. The car was fully operational as even the windows could be raised and lowered.

1940 DeLuxe Six Transparent Sedan

The 1939 transparent Pontiac was probably the most popular vehicle at the World's Fair. In addition, media coverage of the car in various types of magazines was extensive. In short, the car was a tremendous success for the publicity department. What better way to capitalize on this than to produce a 1940 version? After all, the DeLuxe sedan (all-new for 1939) received only minor changes for 1940. Whether the 1939 car was cannibalized to produce the 1940 model is still debatable today, although highly likely. This car was donated to the Smithsonian Institution in 1947, then acquired by two different Pontiac dealers in succession in Pennsylvania and, finally, found its way into the hands of private collectors in the early seventies.

1939 B Body

1940 B Body

1940 Torpedo Eight Transparent Sedan

The General Motors C body is sometimes referred to as the "Cadillac" body, but was also used by the very largest Buick and Oldsmobile models. It is not generally realized that Pontiac shared this same body in 1940, as the Torpedo Eight, and in 1941.

Pontiac built a transparent Torpedo Eight sedan in addition to the DeLuxe Six B body transparent sedan. This new, large, luxurious Pontiac seemed a natural choice for a third transparent car project as it was quite popular. Execution of the Torpedo Eight was of the same high caliber as the previous DeLuxe sedans even to the point of using white for all rubber parts including tires and radiator hoses.

1940 C Body

1941 T9 Tank Proposal

In 1941, Pontiac Division of General Motors proposed building a lightweight tank for the U.S. military. A mockup of this vehicle was produced and contained two six-cylinder flathead Pontiac engines.

Photos of this proposal were recently found in a large metal container in the Pontiac Engineering record storage area, however, no information was found to explain the proposal further. No pictures of a turret mockup were found although it is shown on the drawings. The U.S. Army has no record of this and Marmon-Harrington apparently obtained the production contract for the T9 tank.

T9 Tank

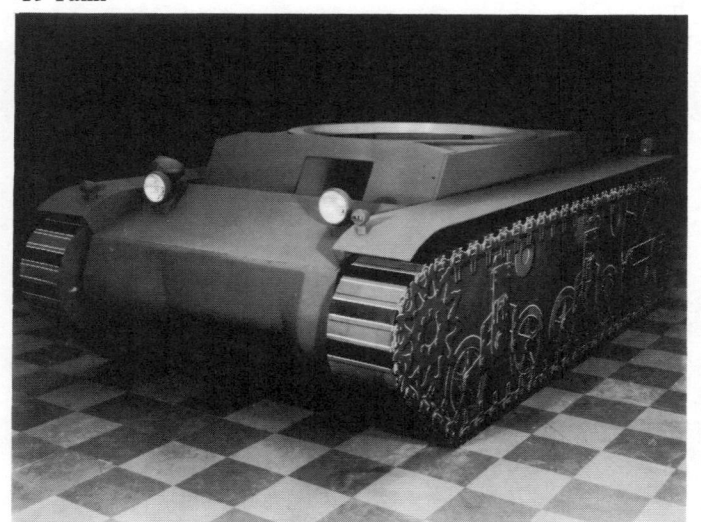

T9 Tank

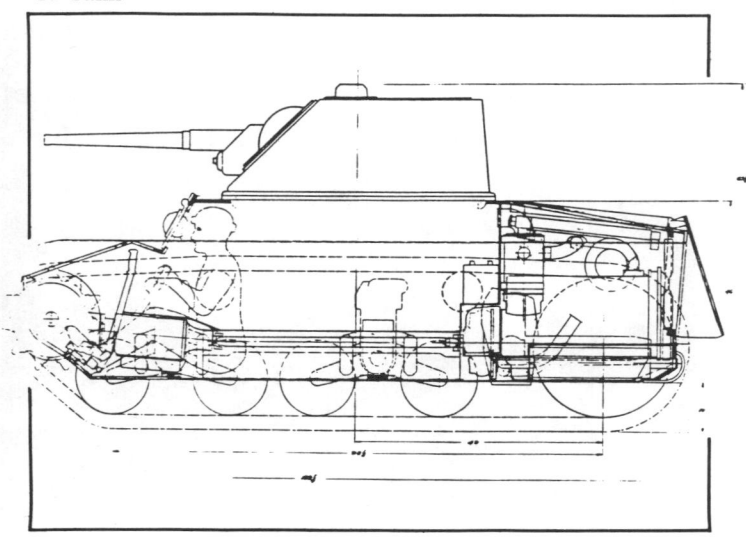

Streamback Trunk Sedan

1940 Special Six Streamback Trunk Sedan

The A-body Pontiac was new for 1940 and renamed the Special Six. Five models were offered including a Business Coupe, Sport Coupe, two-door Touring Sedan, four-door Touring Sedan and custom wood-bodied Station Wagon. A sixth body style, the Streamback Trunk Sedan, was slated for production. At least one was built and displayed at an auto show. The body style was illustrated in the Special Six folder where a price of $876 was quoted. This price was identical to that of the Touring Sedan. For whatever reason, the body style was cancelled at the last moment. An equivalent model in Oldsmobile's 60 series was also planned, but never built.

1949 Catalina

The "hardtop-convertible" styling, introduced by GM in 1949, was an immediate hit. It appeared first as the Buick Riviera, Cadillac Coupe deVille and Olds Holiday. It became obvious that the formula could be successfully applied to the less costly A-body Pontiac and Chevrolet. During 1949, both divisions prepared prototypes although production did not begin until the 1950 model year. The Pontiac version was named the Catalina coupe. The same name was retained when actual production began. The 1949 Catalina looked the same as regular production 1949 Pontiacs except for the distinctive roof. There was no center pillar between the side windows. Consequently, when the windows were rolled down, the car had the appearance of a convertible with a hardtop, hence the name, hardtop-convertible.

Catalina   Catalina

1950 Fleur de Lis

Fleur de Lis

Factory-customized show cars made their appearance during the 1950s. They were a relatively inexpensive way to build one-off show vehicles. Regular production models were given special trim materials, color schemes and sometimes minor body changes. The Fleur de Lis and the Magnificent may have been Pontiac's first customized show cars. Both were built for display at the Canadian National Exposition in Toronto.

In 1950, all Canadian-built Pontiacs were called Fleetleaders. The Fleetleader was a lower-cost line to supplement the American range of Chieftains, Streamliners and Catalinas. They featured coupes and sedans in fastback and trunkback styles and were built on a shorter Chevrolet wheelbase employing many Chevrolet chassis and body parts.

The Fleur de Lis was a specially trimmed Fleetleader fastback four-door sedan. It was painted a delicate gray-white and the same color was used inside on the leather bolsters in conjunction with French blue fabrics.

1950 Magnificent

The Magnificent, also prepared for the Canadian National Exposition, may have been Pontiac's first American-bodied customized show car. It was an imported (from the U.S.) Chieftain four-door sedan with a special green and cream color scheme. The lower body was painted dark metallic green and the top was covered in a crinkle champagne finish. The interior was meticulously color-coordinated with the exterior. Green and cream colored nylon duck fabrics were used for seating upholstery and door panels. Floor carpets were forest green.

With the elapse of over 30 years, much of the significance of the Magnificent has been lost to the casual observer. It should be remembered, however, that metallic paint jobs and color-coordinated interiors were not common features in automobiles of 1950. Most manufacturers (including Pontiac) offered interiors in one color (usually gray or tan) no matter what exterior color was selected. Cars like the Magnificent with colorful interiors stood out when displayed with regular production models.

Magnificent

8

Cutaway

1953 Cutaway

A Chieftain four-door sedan, altered for the 1953 Motorama, was designed to display interior and mechanical aspects simultaneously with the exterior shape of the car. This was the basic premise behind the pre-war Plexiglas cars. In this case, the execution was different. Sections of the passenger compartment were cleverly cut away to expose the engine, transmission, driveline, frame and trunk. Exposed parts were either painted a brilliant duco or chromed to enhance the display. The car appeared intact from the front, rear and driver's side.

Avalon Interior

1953 Avalon

During the early 1950s, Pontiac's Catalina was noted not only for its hardtop styling, but also for its special interior/exterior color coordination. Particularly in the Super Deluxe (or later Custom) models, bright two-toned schemes were meticulously matched inside to outside. In 1953, Pontiac prepared the Avalon, a four-door sedan with the same color coordination as practiced with the two-door Catalinas. Black nylon and chartreuse leather were used inside to match the exterior paint colors. Interior window frames were chromed in the Catalina manner to give some of the hardtop look to this sedan. Even the name had a Catalina connection as Avalon is the village on Santa Catalina Island in California.

X-Ray Car

1954 X-Ray Car

For the 1954 GM Motorama, Pontiac revived a pre-war concept of using a plastic body to showcase the inner workings of a car. Dubbed the X-ray car, a Chieftain four-door sedan was created with a plastic body. The top was white but the rest of the car appeared black. Mounted inside the car at key points were black lights that illuminated various mechanical components. Fluorescent paint was used on these components to enhance the display. The overall effect was like that of an x-ray photograph.

1953 Parisienne

1953 Parisienne

1953 Parisienne

After a two-year absence because of the Korean War, the General Motors Motorama returned in 1953. Its first stop was the Waldorf-Astoria in New York City, a fitting location for the presentation of the Parisienne town car. It was an adaptation of the traditional chauffeur-driven landau carriage. The roof over the rear passenger compartment was fixed. Chauffeur and footman seats in the front were open to the elements, however, a plexiglass dome was provided for inclement weather.

The exterior was painted in what Pontiac termed "black-black", a deeply hand-lacquered finish. The interior was black and pink. Pink leather was used for the headliner, door panels, front bucket seats and steering wheel rim. A vanity case and heater controls were mounted between the front seats for rear passenger use. The rear compartment was upholstered in black dull satin nylon frieze interspersed with aluminum yarns. Carpeting was black broadtail with the dash, steering column and spokes painted black.

Although based on a stock eight-cylinder chassis, the exterior boasted numerous subtle differences over production models. Many of these changes were incorporated into subsequent cars. The most notable of these features was the wraparound windshield with frameless vent windows. These windows never made it to production but the windshield was strikingly similar to that used on the new Pontiac body in 1955. The rear fenders were subtly altered and the large vertical louvers just behind the doors eliminated the chrome splash guards that were found on production models. These splash guards were the last vestiges of separate fender styling as they disappeared altogether in 1955. Since fender skirts were not used on the Parisienne, a small lip was placed around the rear wheel openings to match that of the front. The traditional "Silver Streaks" were absent from the trunk being replaced by the inverted "V" and circle used on later Pontiacs. Initially, the car used the standard chrome headlamp bezels. Later, black "French visored" bezels were used when the car was displayed to the public. Original photos were airbrushed to make this change. The Indian head hood ornament was curiously absent, replaced by an airplane-style ornament not unlike that used on 1955-56 cars. Even the series of three stars associated with later Star Chief models was first seen on the Parisienne front fenders.

1954 Parisienne

10

1954 Parisienne

The 1954 Pontiacs were similar to the 1953 models. The grille and other trim pieces were altered for the annual model change and the Parisienne received a similar update. The grille and parking lights were changed to the 1954 style and the only other exterior change was the paint color. Silver-blue replaced black. The interior was changed to harmonize with the exterior. The dash and steering wheel matched the silver-blue exterior. White leather replaced pink and a silver-gray plush rug replaced the broadtail of the year before. The changes outlined above were relatively simple and inexpensive and allowed Pontiac an extra year of promotional display for the Parisienne.

1954 Parisienne

1954 Bonneville Special

Pontiac unveiled the Bonneville Special, the division's first sporty dream car, at the General Motors Motorama in January, 1954. The car was an immediate sensation in New York and later Miami. It garnered so much attention for Pontiac that a second vehicle was built. This allowed it to be shown simultaneously at the Motorama in Los Angeles and the auto show in Detroit.

The Bonneville Special's roof was made of transparent Plexiglas, dubbed the "bubble canopy". Twin counter-balanced gull-wing type panels were hinged at the center of the roof. Once these panels were raised, the doors were opened from inside. There were no exterior door handles. Since the cockpit was completely closed while in motion, ventilation was provided by two air intakes on the cowl. Controls for the ventilation were mounted on the tunnel between the seats which also housed the ignition switch and Hydramatic gear selector. The interior featured twin bucket seats upholstered in copper-red leather and a three-spoked, competition-type steering wheel. A brushed aluminum instrument panel housed the gauges, including a tachometer. All instruments were black-lighted from a source mounted on the canopy center panel. A clock and compass were mounted on the windshield header and behind the seats was a tool compartment. The flooring was a grid-type with rubber inserts.

Outside, the fiberglass body was painted metallic copper-red. Headlights were recessed with transparent plastic covers. The bumperettes below the headlights were attached to the frame, not the body as they appeared to be. Aluminum vent moldings on the front fender were nonfunctional. The wheels were brushed aluminum discs with turbine-like fins and chrome knock-off hubs. The car was powered by the Pontiac Straight 8 engine with four carburetors. It rode on a 100-inch wheelbase with an overall length of 158.3 inches and height a mere 48.5 inches. Since the car was named after the Bonneville Salt Flats outside of Salt Lake City, General Motors obtained a set of license plates from Utah Governor J. Bracken Lee reading "GM 000 Utah 1954".

It seems that General Motors may have considered producing sports cars at other divisions besides Chevrolet. The Bonneville Special appeared about one year after Chevy introduced the first Corvette. It was about this time that Oldsmobile and Buick displayed their two-passenger show cars (F-88 and Wildcat, respectively). All three of the B-O-P experimental sports cars borrowed heavily from Corvette's basic styling themes. Corvette sales were very sluggish the first few years. For this reason, GM executives may have considered the sports car market too limited to justify production at the other divisions. One of these cars exists in private hands in Michigan today.

1954 Strato Streak

The Strato Streak was originally built for the 1954 General Motors Motorama and was shown in conjunction with the Bonneville Special sports car. The Strato Streak was billed as a "spectator sports car", the perfect car to carry four passengers to sporting events. Shown one year before the arrival of four-door hardtops, the car featured characteristics of the soon-to-be-announced models. An extra rigid frame served as the foundation for a four-door sedan with no center pillars. When both side doors were opened, there was no obstruction between the front and rear passenger compartments. To accomplish this feat, the back doors were hinged at the rear (sometimes referred to as suicide doors when in general use before the war due to their proneness to being sucked open at high speed by air pressure). Special locks were installed on the rear doors so that they opened only when the car was stopped and the transmission in neutral. This unique door design also eliminated the step-over sill accomplished by setting the sill, back and extending the door sheetmetal over the road clearance level.

The interior featured four bucket seats. The driver's seat and front passenger seat swiveled 90 degrees for ease of entrance and exit. A center console housed windshield wiper and washer controls, heater controls, radio, cigar lighter and ashtray. Glove compartments for front and rear passengers were also mounted in the console. Interior ventilation was provided by twin cowl intakes below the windshield and air was extracted through outlets above the rear window. A pair of levers on each side of the steering column controlled air.

1955 Star Chief Custom Safari

Although not a "special edition" in the same sense as others in this book, the 1955 Star Chief Safari was very special indeed. It was announced as a mid-year model and was priced significantly higher than other Pontiacs of that year. It was the only Star Chief model on the shorter wheelbase chassis and the only Pontiac wagon with Pontiac-style rear fenders. Other 1955 Pontiac station wagons used Chevrolet rear fenders with Pontiac taillights mounted in them. Color choices were limited to brown and ivory or turquoise and ivory (or a solid paint job in any of these three). The interior used the Custom leather trim in the same two-toned shades as the outside. The cargo area was carpeted and featured chrome skid strips. Seven vertical chrome strips were mounted on the outside of the tailgate. This Safari was easily the lowest volume Pontiac model of 1955 as only 3,760 were built. This car, along with the 1956 and 1957 versions, were the first Pontiacs to receive Milestone Car recognition.

1955 Strato Star

The 1955 Strato Star was one of the most practical dream cars ever produced by Detroit. It featured exceptional visibility and accessibility. The passenger compartment was almost entirely surrounded by glass. Roof support pillars were very narrow and the rear side windows wrapped around the back of the car. The rear pillars started as ridges on the roof and extended out onto the rear deck as small fins. They served as roof supports through the back window.

Accessibility was highlighted when either of the doors was opened, a six-inch panel in the roof flipped up to allow easier entrance or exit. It returned to the closed position electrically. As in all two-door cars, access to the rear seat was by folding the front seatback forward. In the Strato Star, the seatback was in three sections instead of the customary two as the center section was stationary. This allowed passengers to enter the rear compartment from both sides simultaneously. The clock was mounted above the windshield for all passengers to view.

The Strato Star was painted metallic silver and trimmed in Vermillion red. The unusually large cutout wheels were red as were the air slots in the wheels. The interior used red vinyl on the seats, door panels and dash with brushed aluminum accents. The car was powered by a four-barrel version of the 287 cubic inch Pontiac V-8 engine. Wheelbase was 120 inches and height was 53 inches.

There may have been some controversy or confusion over the name of the car as the Strato Star is occasionally referred to as the Strato Chief in various Pontiac publications. In some press releases of the car (with pictures clearly indicating "Strato Star" on the front fender), it was called the Strato Chief. The confusion is compounded historically by a series of Pontiacs built in Canada from 1958 through 1970 named the Strato Chief.

1956 Club de Mer

The Club de Mer sports car was probably Pontiac's most famous show car. It was one of the biggest crowd-pleasers of the 1956 Motorama. Revell even made a scale model kit of the car. It was Pontiac's second two-passenger sports car in three years.

The Cerulean blue, brushed aluminum body was extremely low-slung. It had only 5 inches of ground clearance and measured a mere 38.4 inches high. Unique styling features combined with these low dimensions achieved a sleek sporty appearance. The front and rear were designed without bumpers with only thin chrome moldings in their place. Twin bubble windshields were provided for each passenger. A single dorsal fin was mounted on the center of the rear deck and headlamps and parking lamps were hidden behind revolving doors.

The Vermillion red interior featured two leather bucket seats separated by a center console. This console housed the transmission shift lever, ignition, radio and deck lid opening lever. Other control levers were mounted on the driver's door.

The Club de Mer incorporated a number of mechanical features in line with the sporty concept of the car. Pontiac's 317 cubic inch Strato Streak V-8 engine was modified with two four-barrel carburetors to develop over 300 hp. The 3-speed synchromesh transmission was mounted at the rear axle (a feature later used on 1961-63 Tempest and LeMans models). Air outlet ports were mounted on the cowl at the end of the Silver Streaks to eliminate hot air buildup under the hood. Dual exhausts (a new production option for 1956) were employed with twin extensions mounted to either side of the rear license plate.

The novelty shot above was issued by GM using a model evidently built by GM Design (not the Revell model mentioned in the text).

1956 Star Chief Custom Safari

The 1956 Star Chief Custom Safari was similar to the 1955 model, but featured a different grille and side trim and a larger engine. The color choices were changed slightly as the turquoise was darker and the brown was lighter. Only 4,042 of these wagons were built for 1956. Again, this was the lowest volume model of any Pontiac for the year.

1957 Star Chief Custom Safari

The final year for the two-door Star Chief Custom Safari was 1957. Only 1,292 were built for the year, making it the rarest of the three model years. The front and rear ends were restyled and the color choices were expanded. After more than 20 years, the chrome Silver Streaks were removed from the hood. The engine was enlarged to 347 cubic inches.

In mid-year, a four-door version of the Safari made its appearance. Based on the standard wagon body, the four-door was sometimes referred to as the "four-door" Safari and sometimes as the "Transcontinental." In trim and quality it was essential the same as the two-door model.

1956 Safari

1957 Safari

1957 Transcontinental Safari

17

1957 Bonneville Convertible

The first Bonneville available to the public was a true limited edition. Only 630 were built, all convertibles. The major feature of the car was the fuel-injected 347 cubic inch Pontiac V-8 engine. This small batch of cars was built to put the fuel injection engines in the field for hands-on testing. The engine was not offered in any other Pontiac in 1957. Fuel injection became a production option in 1958, although it was a different system than that offered in 1957. Ultimately, the Tri-Power engine offered similar and more reliable performance so the fuel injection engine was discontinued entirely. The Bonneville was built on the longer Star Chief body and included all-leather Custom interior trim used on Star Chief Customs of that year. Note that the Star Chief convertible was not available with this Custom trim, although other Star Chief body styles were. There was a distinctive side treatment for the Bonneville not shared with others. The side spear was similar to other models, but included a much larger chrome bullet in the rear fender. The fender also included a ribbed chrome splash guard behind the rear wheel opening and "BONNEVILLE" lettering at the top. The front fenders featured matching block lettering spelling out "FUEL INJECTION" and a series of seven fake louvers. Standard equipment level was very high as was the price of $5,782. This was close to twice the base price of a Star Chief convertible and $700 more than a Cadillac Series 62 convertible for that year. Today, that would equate with a $30,000 Pontiac!

The original Bonneville. Pontiac General Manager Semon Knudsen appears at the far right in the shot below.

1957 Jan Krebs Star Chiefs

In 1957, Pontiac was paying particular attention to feminine taste in designing their cars. Pontiac gave free reign to its sole woman designer, Jan Krebs, to create two special Star Chiefs.

The first car was a convertible painted chiffon pink with a magenta red spear. The interior was upholstered in a matching metallic pink leather. A red and pink nylon fabric was used on the driver's seat as well as on the right rear seat area and the floor was covered with a pink carpeting. The glove compartment contained a lift-out vanity in matching leather along with a note pad and tissue dispenser.

The second Krebs creation was a two-door hardtop painted Onyx black (including the side spear) with an entirely black interior. Both calf grain leather and patent leather were used in the seats. Black mouton was used for the floor carpeting. A monochromatic black car is commonplace today, yet, during the two-toned fifties, it may have been as strange as the pink and red convertible today.

Jan Krebs & her Star Chief

1957 La Parisienne

Together with the fuel-injected Bonneville and the four-door Transcontinental Safari, the La Parisienne was featured in the 1957 Pontiac auto show displays. Unlike the other two, however, the La Parisienne was never built as a production model, even in reduced numbers (as was the limited edition Bonneville). This fact was never made clear in the "Three Surprises" auto show borchure issued by the division for the three cars, and the La Parisienne may have been slated for some sort of production, then scrubbed. This is especially possible as the La Parisienne was the nearest to stock of the three. Really all it was was a Star Chief four-door hardtop with a vinyl roof, an idea later to gain tremendous popularity throughout the industry. In this instance, the vinyl roof was Pearlescent White with a coral lower body color and a two-tone interior of White Pearl and Coral Mist upholstery.

1957 La Parisienne

1958 Bonneville Indianapolis 500 Pace Car

Bonneville Pace Car

The 1958 Indianapolis 500 was paced by a Bonneville convertible. This was a dealer-sponsored car, as opposed to the Pontiac Motor Division sponsorship of 1980 and 1984. The car featured the 300 hp Tri-Power motor.

1958 Golden Jubilee Star Chief

General Motors celebrated its 50th anniversary in 1958. Each division built a limited number of anniversary editions using a special gold color of the new Lucite Acrylic Lacquer. Pontiac built an undeterminable number of Star Chiefs with this color and white side spears.

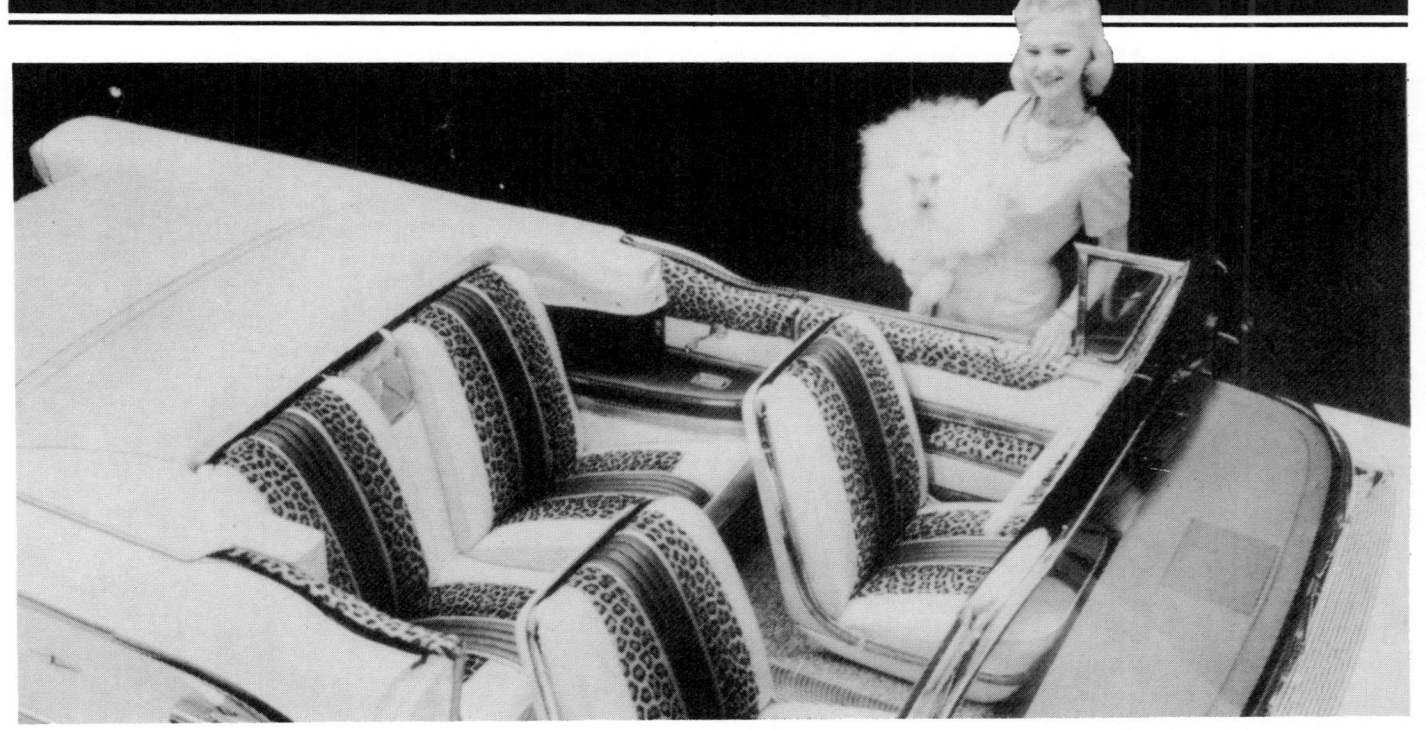

Bonneville Convertible

1958 Bonneville Convertible

Pontiac built a specially trimmed Bonneville convertible for the 1958 Detroit Auto Show. The car was painted golden cameo and its interior featured the newly introduced front bucket seats. Accent panels in the seats and door panels were genuine leopard skin.

A plethora of specially trimmed stock cars was fostered by the exhibition rules at the Detroit show which prohibited experimental type vehicles. Pontiac, along with other GM divisions, reached a zenith with these cars in the early sixties. In some years, Pontiac alone would produce a half dozen of such vehicles.

1959 Star Chief Cutaway

A specially prepared Star Chief Vista, similar in concept to the 1953 cutaway Chieftain sedan, was cut away to reveal its inner features. Parts of the right front fender and hood were cut to expose the engine. Both righthand-side tires, wheels and brakes were sectioned to show their inner workings. The right rear fender and trunk lid were cut out to show the cavernous trunk. The doors on the right side were removed and part of the roof and floor were cut away to show the driveline. Even the seats were cut in half exposing the springs and foam rubber. This intriguing way of opening up the car allowed for the front, rear and driver's side views to remain intact.

Cutaway

1959 Bonneville X-400

A one-off high performance convertible was built for 1959 dubbed the Bonneville X-400. Built on the shorter Catalina body, it featured the higher level Bonneville trim. Bonneville style rear fender trim was not used as simple block letters spelled out "BONNEVILLE X-400" instead. The same style letters were used on the front fenders to spell "SUPERCHARGED", indicating a supercharged 389 cubic inch engine. Exhaust outlets were mounted in the rear fenders, behind the wheel openings. The unique front grille styling featured hidden headlamps and three stars mounted in each grille cavity. This car was apparently the first application of the eight-lug aluminum wheel which became a regular production option in 1960. This car also appears to be the first in a series of at least five X-400 show cars.

In June, 1959, a Pontiac Catalina convertible was reworked by the GM Styling Studio for the personal use of Mrs. Harley Earl, the wife of GM's long-time head of styling. The fact that the car was completed so late in the model year indicates it was not for the auto show circuit. All of the 1959 auto shows would have been over by June. The color choice indicates a feminine character as it was painted pearlescent rose pink. The interior featured pink and white leather upholstery with plum-colored padded dash, carpeting and trunk lining. Officially carrying the Catalina convertible model number (2167), the car had Bonneville level trim (including the bucket seats). The dash even sported the "Bonneville" script nameplate. Exterior trim followed the stock Catalina style with two exceptions: there was no Catalina script on the rear fenders and the larger Bonneville/Star Chief taillamps were used. The obvious attempt was to create a short wheelbase Bonneville convertible in the same vein as 1958. The only short wheelbase Bonneville in production for 1959 was the Safari. Pontiac's resident historian, John Sawruk, thinks the car may have been the altered X-400 convertible. This car is now in private hands.

1960 Bonneville X-400

The 1960 Bonneville X-400 was similar in concept to the 1959 model. It was a short wheelbase Bonneville convertible, although there were no 27 series convertibles in production for 1960. The only 27 series model was the short wheelbase Bonneville Safari. (The long wheelbase Bonnevilles were 28 series models.) The supercharged 389 V-8 was again the driving force under the hood. The eight-lug aluminum wheels were used again, but the hidden headlamps were not. In fact, a stock grille was employed. The only unusual styling feature were special headlamps and the hood ornament. This same style ornament was used again on the first Grand Prix X-400 in 1962. The car was finished in metallic blue with a matching interior. This car still exists in private hands.

1961 XP-758

The XP-758 was an experimental car developed by Pontiac in 1961 as a personal luxury car proposal, similar in concept to the Ford Thunderbird. It was a sporty four-passenger car somewhat smaller than a full-sized Pontiac of that year. Pontiac's resident historian, John Sawruk, thinks this may have been Pontiac's proposal for the E-car. The E-car was GM's answer to the four-passenger Thunderbird in the early sixties. Cadillac was initially approached about building the car, but turned it down. GM management then threw the project open to the other divisions. The XP-758 was probably Pontiac's bid for the car. Buick eventually won approval to build the first E-car which bowed for 1963 as the Riviera. Note that Pontiac's XP-758 is far sportier than the more formal 1963 Riviera. The roofline is semi-fastback and the rear fenders and bumper are very similar to those of the 1961 Jaguar XKE.

1961 Supercharged LeMans

Pontiac debuted the unorthodox Y-body Tempest for 1961. The initial sedan and station wagon were supplemented mid-year with a coupe. A sporty version, dubbed the LeMans, was created for the show circuit and served a dual purpose. It drew attention to the new Tempest coupe and tested public reaction to a sporty Tempest.
The LeMans modifications were in three general areas. The upgraded monochromatic interior featured front bucket seats, a GMC supercharger was bolted to the standard four-cylinder engine and genuine wire wheels and a louvered hood were used to spice up the exterior styling.
Public reaction to the LeMans was so favorable that a production version, along with a convertible model, reached dealer showrooms with the 1962 model introduction. The attractive interior was left intact, however, the supercharger, wire wheels and louvered hood were dropped.

1962 LeMans GT

The first LeMans GT was not built in 1972, but, in fact, 10 years earlier. In 1962, Pontiac applied to the Federation Internationale de L'Automobile to have a 389 LeMans GT recognized in the Grand Touring category for international racing events. At least one model of such a car was built. Standard LeMans power was a 194.5 cubic inch, four-cylinder engine (literally half of a 389 V-8). The 326 Pontiac V-8 was made available in the transaxle LeMans in 1963, but the 389 was not fitted to regular production cars until the larger conventional LeMans arrived in 1964. Then it was called the GTO. The only appearance change on the 1962 389 LeMans GT was the large scoop on the hood.

1961 Alligator Jaw Tempest

The big news at Pontiac in 1961 was the dramatically new Tempest, a car that had so many engineering features it was almost impossible to list them all. So, apparently, the division decided to *show* them. This car, which was actually Tempest serial number one, was similar in concept to the 1941 alligator show car, only the entire body opened, rather than just the front half, as in 1941. The Alligator Jaw Temptest was painted Shelltone Ivory with a ted and ivory custom interior.

1962 Grand Marque

The Grand Marque was a specially trimmed red-bronze firefrost convertible used for the show circuit. Built on the B-body, the exterior was a conglomeration of current year trim pieces. It used the Catalina/ Star Chief grille, Bonneville side trim and Star Chief taillights and rear trim. Double-ring whitewall tires were used with the production aluminum wheels. Eight-lug aluminum wheel fanciers will note this was the first car to have the insets painted. Production units were painted starting in 1964.

The interior featured the Bonneville dash and console with unique door panels and seat design. The seats were upholstered in a combination of leather and fabric and the floor and lower door panels were covered with mouton carpet. The door panels used longer armrests with paddle-type handles. Like the painted aluminum wheels, these appeared on production Pontiacs in 1964 (Bonneville Brougham). Also of note were the electrically-operated vent windows, an option that didn't show up in the accessory catalogue until 1963.

1961-2 Monte Carlo

Pontiac had not attempted a two-passenger roadster since the 1956 Club de Mer. For 1961, the division used the compact Y-body Tempest convertible to fashion a roadster derivation called the Monte Carlo. Fifteen inches were lopped off between the door and rear wheel opening thereby eliminating room for the rear seat. This brought wheelbase down to 97 inches and overall length to 175 inches. The unique curved driveshaft had to be shortened to accommodate the revised bodywork.

A supercharged 195 cubic inch four-cylinder engine powered the car through the standard 4-speed transaxle gearbox. This drivetrain was also featured on the 1961 LeMans show car.

The stock 15-inch wheels were replaced with a 14-inch magnesium type to lower the overall stance. Around the driver's compartment was a low windshield and built-in headrests in the deck lid. These further enhanced the low appearance of the car. Other exterior highlights included a deep-set 1961 style grille, hood louvers (a la 1961 LeMans show car) and stainless steel cowlings over the side fender coves. The inboard headlamps were special driving lights.

The interior featured two blue leather bucket seats with retracting seat belts. A full-length floor console of brushed aluminum was mounted between the seats. A vacuum pressure gauge was placed on the console and a special instrument cluster, including tachometer, was incorporated into the standard Tempest dash. The blue floor carpeting featured chrome skid strips.

The exterior was painted pearlescent white with twin blue stripes on the hood and rear deck. This color combination returned in 1969 on the first Trans Am.

The attention understandably being concentrated on the new Tempest may account for the absence of a full-size X-400 show car in 1961. The 1961-2 Monte Carlo still exists.

1962 X-400 Grand Prix

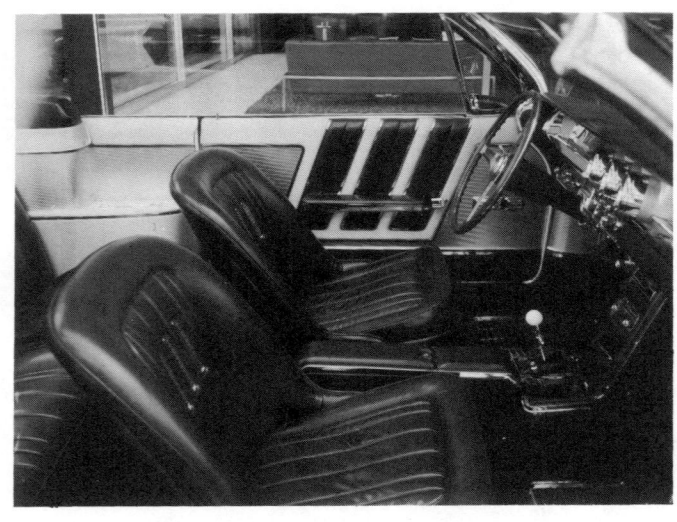

It is commonly acknowledged that Pontiac produced Grand Prix convertibles only in the 1967 model year. This is not exactly true. In the early 1960s, a series of experimental Grand Prix convertibles were built, each named X-400.

As a styling exercise, the X-400 represented subtle changes over the production model. Replacing the quad round headlights were two rectangular units with flip-up wire grilles. The twin fender ornaments were replaced by a unique center hood ornament. Twin grille vents were added to the hood along with the letters "SUPERCHARGED", giving away the 4-71 GMC supercharger underneath. A fiberglass boot covered the top when lowered and aluminum trim was placed in the side coved area. Dual bullet-shaped rear view mirrors were mounted on each door and the GP plaque was absent from the left grille.

The red and white interior featured unique bucket seats and door panel trim, matching the red exterior. The dash was basically that of the production 1962 GP although three round gauges angled toward the driver were mounted in the spot normally occupied by the radio. The three gauges were a tachometer, a supercharger boost pressure gauge and a clock. The radio was, in turn, mounted in the console which was totally unlike the production version. The console also housed two levers: the 4-speed transmission shift and the lever to select three degrees of quietness in the dual exhaust system. This unique exhaust system had its rear outlets mounted in the lower rear fenders.

1963 X-400 Grand Prix

A second Grand Prix-based X-400 convertible was built in 1963 carrying over many of the features used on the original 1962 model. It featured a supercharged 421 cubic inch V-8 engine, hood scoops with the letters "SUPER-CHARGED", grille-covered rectangular headlamps, fiberglass top boot, wood steering wheel and bullet-shaped outside rear view mirrors.

There were other changes besides the restyled sheetmetal. The color combination was pearlescent yellow with black pinstriping, twin scoops were cut into the rear fenders and exhaust outlets were moved from the rear fenders to just behind the doors in front of the rear wheels. Also new was a brushed aluminum rocker panel molding extending from the front to the rear of the car.

A third Grand Prix-based X-400 was built in 1964 and first appeared at the Chicago Auto Show. It was a reworked version of the 1963 car and still exists in private hands.

1963 LeMans Marque

Just as there were two Grand Marques based on the Bonneville for 1963, there were two LeMans Marques for that year also. One car was painted saddle firefrost with matching interior. As in the Bonneville version, the floor carpet, kickpads and top boot were brown and white calf-skin. The other car was painted gold firefrost with white and gold interior. The carpet was white. All other features of both cars were stock 1963 LeMans.

1963 Bonneville Grand Marque III

Two Bonneville Grand Marque III convertibles were built in 1963. One was painted saddle firefrost with matching interior. The unique feature of this car was the use of brown and white calf skin for the carpeting, lower door panels and convertible top boot.

The other Grand Marque III used a white interior with white pouff carpeting. On the exterior, it featured wire wheels with three-ring whitewall tires.

All other features of both cars were stock 1963 Bonneville.

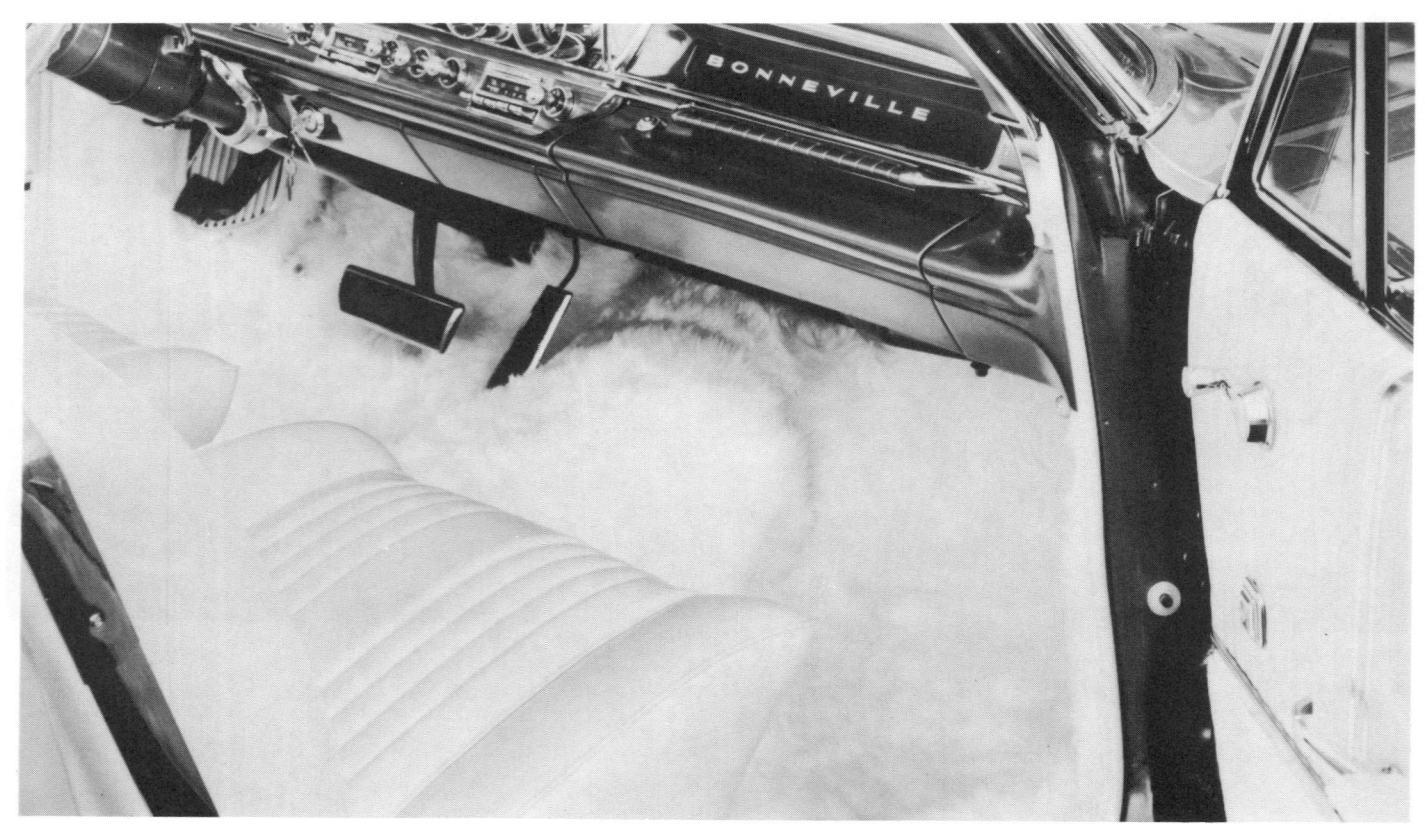

1963 Fleur de Lis

The Fleur de Lis incorporated the heraldic three-petal iris emblem into this special LeMans convertible show car. On the outside, a rich pearl mauve paint color approximating that of the iris was used. Special Fleur de Lis plaques, including the insignia, were mounted on the front fenders and, as was customary at the time for convertible show cars, a fiberglass top boot replaced the vinyl.

The basic interior color combination used was the mauve color scheme, although red and black triangular accent panels and fleur de lis emblems were used on the seats. A unique diagonal seat pattern, similar to that used on the 1965 LeMans, was first shown here as well. The door panels were also somewhat different from the regular LeMans version as they were upholstered to the window level instead of using a metal sill. Longer armrests with paddle-type door handles were used but most notable was the use of carpet on the door. Instead of being at the bottom of the door to be used as a kick-pad, it was used in the center of the door totally surrounding the armrest.

1963 Maharani

The Maharani was a specially trimmed aqua Bonneville convertible prepared for the 1963 show circuit. The most notable feature was the use of peacock feathers on the interior door panels. The unique door panel design also encompassed longer armrests with paddle-type door handles and combined electric window controls for all side windows as well as vent windows. Although the interior was basically aqua, the leather-covered seats used a rainbow of colors for each individual panel. The rear featured two separate bucket seats matching the ones in front. Luxurious pouff carpeting also distinguished the Maharani from production Bonnevilles.

A turquoise pearl paint job and fiberglass convertible top boot were the distinctive exterior features. The Maharani nameplate replaced the Bonneville on the front fenders and dashboard, but not on the grille or rear deck lid.

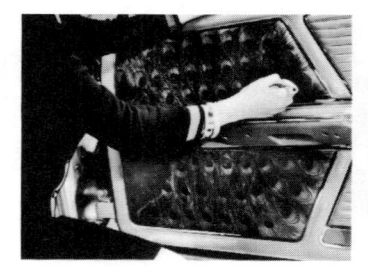

1964 Clam

Not since the 1959 cutaway Star Chief had Pontiac built a show car to display internal features. Built for a series of displays and winding up at the New York World's Fair, was a special Grand Prix. It was nicknamed the "Clam" as it was cut on a horizontal plane and designed to open up like a clam shell. A hydraulic tilt mechanism tilted the car toward the viewer as it opened, displaying the engine compartment, interior and trunk. The car returned to its four wheels as the body closed.

1964 Flamme

There is some confusion regarding the Flamme convertibles of 1964. Official factory photographs show two obviously different cars although never together. It could be that there was only one car altered from a LeMans to a GTO.

Both versions used the same interior. Seats and door panels were upholstered in red leather and lame fabric in a unique design different from stock models. The dash and door panels featured aluminum plating behind the dials and armrests and walnut accents were used in the lower dash.

The LeMans Flamme was displayed at the Chicago Auto Show. Other than interior modifications, a candy apple red paint job and GTO hood scoops, the car looked like a regular production LeMans convertible.

The GTO Flamme exterior was altered more extensively than the LeMans model. Rectangular headlights replaced the four round stock units. Lettering was removed from the grille and the hood scoops were blacked out. A pinstripe was added to the top of the fenders and doors and the stock rocker panel molding was replaced by a unique ribbed scuff plate below each door. The engine exhaust pipes were shortened so that the outlets were moved to just behind the front wheels. Reversed chrome wheels replaced the standard ones.

GTO Flamme

LeMans Flamme

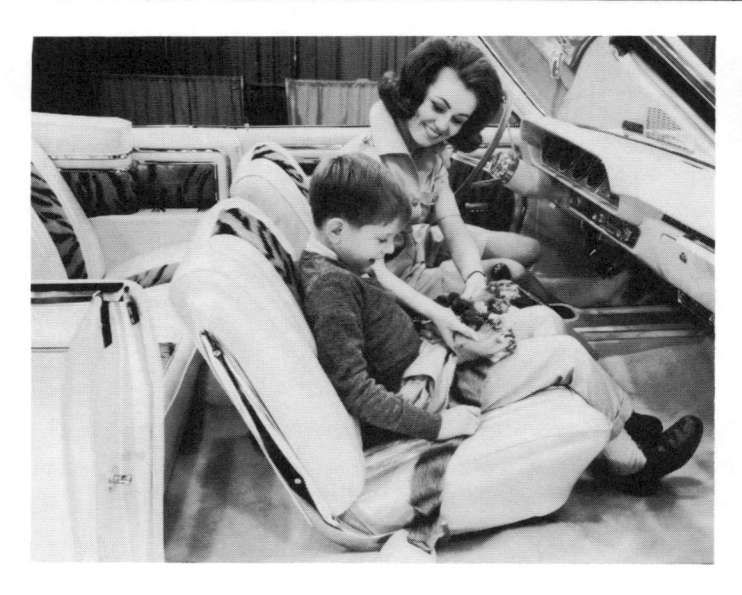

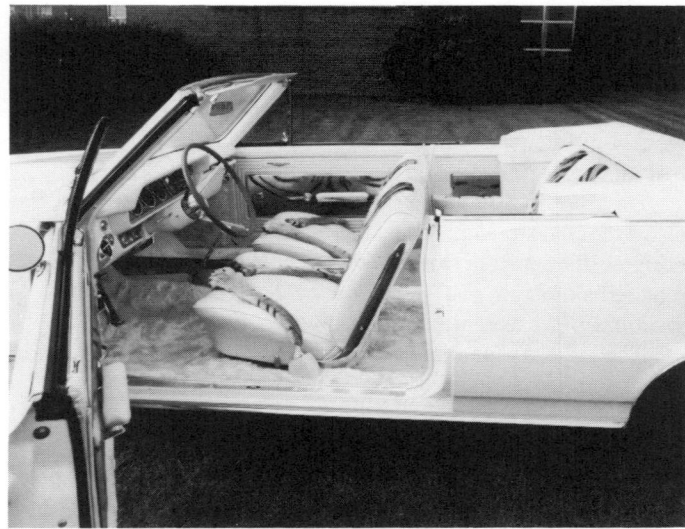

1965 GTO Tiger

In 1965, two separate Tiger projects were undertaken based on the GTO convertible. The first was strictly an exterior exercise, and a ludicrous one at best. The car was painted orange with black tiger stripes, a tiger's face was painted on the hood with three-dimensional eyes and a tail was added to the trunk lid. A Tempest/LeMans hood was used sans hood scoops.

The second Tiger project was strictly an interior exercise using four genuine tiger skins for accents. The factory released photographs showed two variations on this theme. In both cases, seat belts for the front bucket seats were covered with the tiger fur. In fact, the actual tiger paws were used to cover the buckles! In one exercise, the standard GTO interior was used with fur panels inserted in the seatbacks and door and side panels. In the other, a unique seat pattern combined the tiger fur and leather on the seats. Special door and side panels were created using larger sections of the tiger fur.

1966 Grand Corniche

The 1966 Grand Corniche was an update of the 1953-54 Parisienne. That concept was a chauffeur-driven two-door with a fixed roof over the rear seat to protect the passengers and an open top over the front seat for the driver. This created the elegant appeal of the town cars of the 1920s and 1930s.

Based on the 1966 Grand Prix, and named after the famous Mediterranean coastal highway, the Grand Corniche was almost totally aqua. This color choice was meant to accent the water image of the name. The exterior paint was pearl aqua with an aqua Cordova top. The interior was matching aqua with leather upholstery on the front bucket seats and a combination of leather and cloth on the rear bench seat. The aqua was even carried to the tires, which featured three aqua stripes instead of the usual single white band. The wheels were a nonproduction wire type.

1966 Banshee and XP-833

Pontiac celebrated its 40th anniversary in 1966. Perhaps in commemoration of this, the division built a gran turismo show car completely unrelated to any production model. In fact, this was the first such nonproduction-based show car in 10 years (since the Club de Mer in 1956). Named the Banshee, after the Marine jet fighter plane, the car was a worthy successor to the Club de Mer.

The Banshee was smaller than any production Pontiac of 1966. Wheelbase was 109 inches, overall length was 196.7 inches and height was a scant 49.8 inches. In comparison, the wheelbase and length figures for a Tempest of that year were 115 and 206.4 inches, respectively. The Banshee's dimensions compared more closely with the yet-to-be-announced 1967 Firebird, which rode on a 108.1-inch wheelbase with 188.8 inches of overall length.

The Banshee not only previewed future Firebird dimensions, but many of its styling themes as well. The one-piece bumper-grille and the rear taillight and bumper effect were similar in concept to the 1967 Firebird. The one-panel side glass and fastback roofline were later picked up in the 1970 Firebird. Other features of the Banshee that showed up in subsequent production Pontiacs were concealed windshield wipers and the elimination of vent windows. Four large air scoops under the windshield replaced them on the Banshee.

The Banshee boasted features that never made it to production. The most notable of these were the unique doors. They were 63 inches long (about 20 inches longer than conventional doors) and slid open parallel to the car rather than swinging away from it. They were counterbalanced to rise when opened to clear sidewalk curbs. In addition, two gull-winged flippers in the top popped up for easy access, especially to the rear seats. The front fenders and hood were an unusual one-piece design hinged at the front to pivot as a single unit. The headlights retracted into the hood. The interior featured four bucket seats, the rear two folding down for increased storage space. There was no trunk opening on the rear deck and all access to the storage area behind the seats was through the passenger compartment (a la Corvette). A stock 421 cubic inch engine powered the car, but the driveline was a nonstock torque tube design. The Banshee also featured independent rear suspension.

Sometimes confused with the Banshee are the XP-833 prototypes. The XP-833 was a two-passenger sports car project Pontiac developed in the mid-sixties. It was killed by GM brass before its planned 1966 announcement. Prior to this, six vehicles were actually built. The last two were built with fiberglass bodies from the Dow-Smith Co. as fully operational cars. One was an OHC six convertible, one a V-8 hardtop (with a removable top). They were subsequently sold to Pontiac employees. The surviving hardtop is silver, the convertible is white.

The exterior styling was similar to the Banshee show car, especially at the front end. Even the dash panels inside were very similar. The Banshee nameplate was applied to one of the early mock-ups and later added to the surviving hardtop XP-833 by owner Bill Collins.

The XP-833 prototypes were significantly different in concept from the Banshee. Fundamentally, they were two-passenger cars whereas the Banshee was a four-place vehicle. This resulted in smaller dimensions. Wheelbase was only 90 inches and overall length was 167.7 inches making it about 2 1/2 feet shorter than the Banshee. Overall weight was 2,200 pounds.

1966 Banshee

XP-833

XP-833

XP-833 Interior

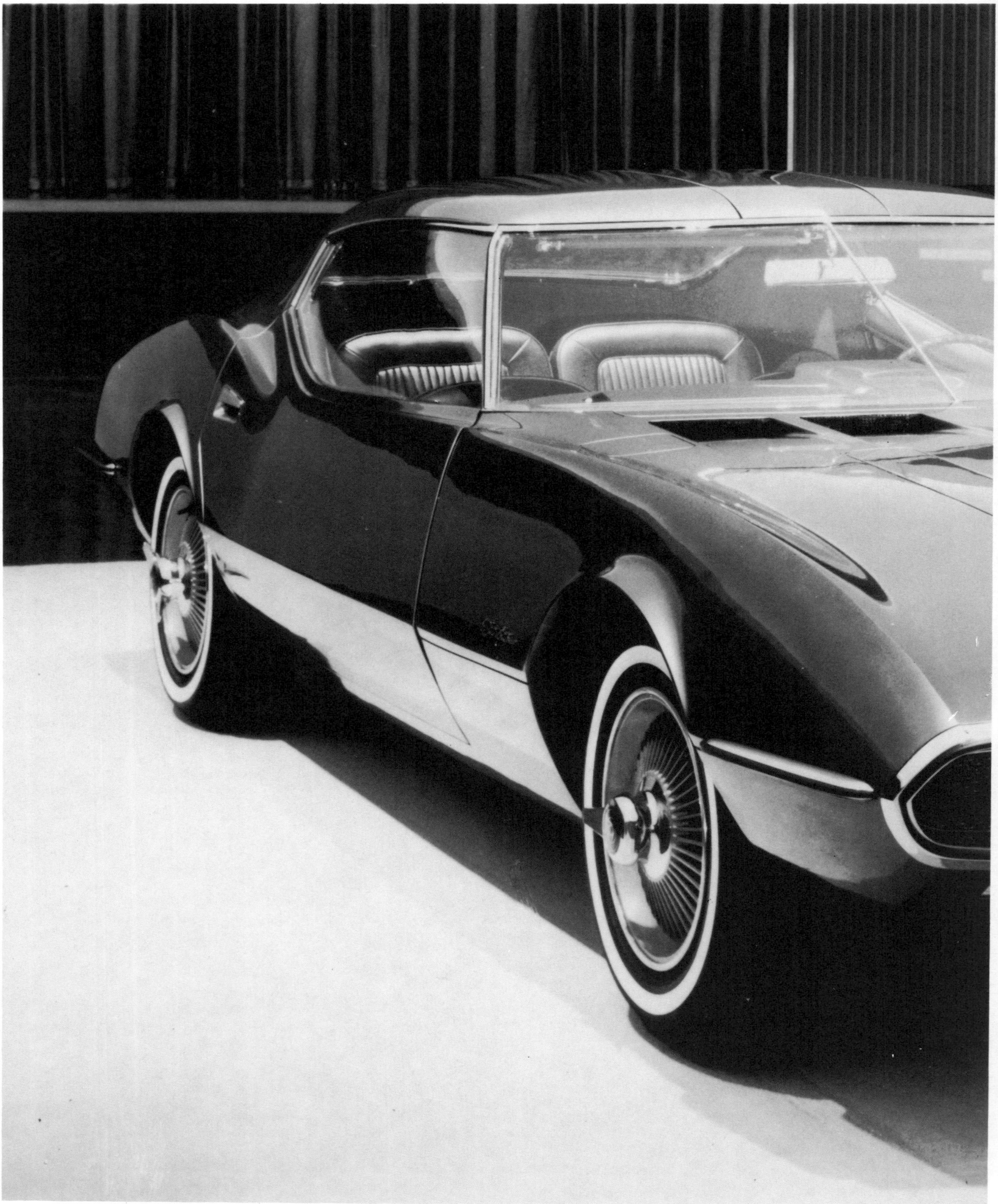

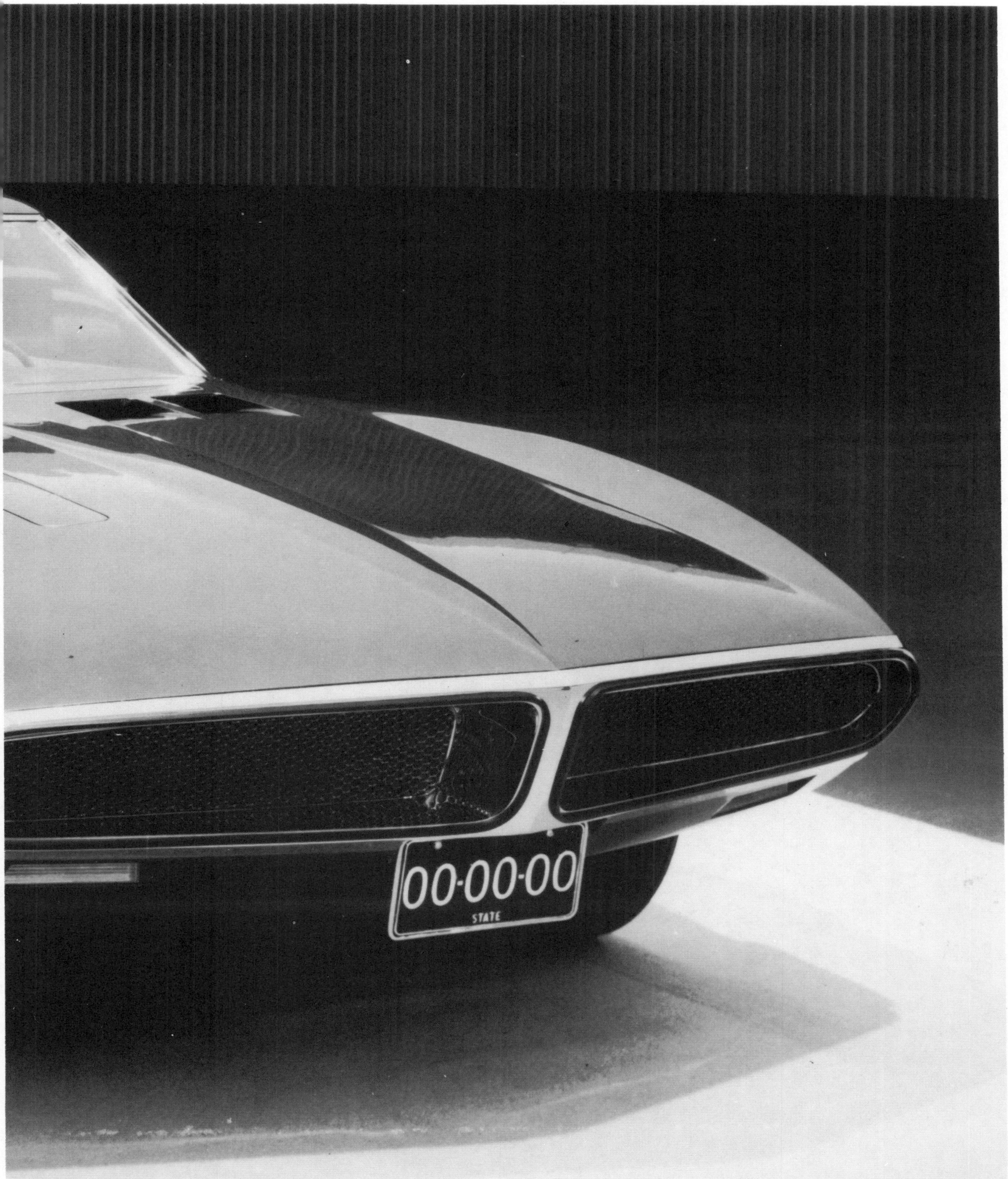
00-00-00
STATE

1967 Grand Prix St. Moritz

Following Pontiac's 1967 theme of sports-oriented show cars was the St. Moritz. The St. Moritz carried the snow skiing theme to a Grand Prix convertible. This was the first, and ultimately, the only year Pontiac built Grand Prix convertibles (except for the earlier X-400 show cars).

The interior was upholstered in a combination of leather and cloth. The leather was used on the seat bolsters and door panels in an ice blue color. The seat and door panel inserts were actual Swiss handwoven sweater-style fabric.

The exterior was painted a matching high pearlescent ice blue. For the St. Moritz, the side pinstriping was moved to the leading edge of the side panels (halfway down the fenders and doors). On production Grand Prixs, the stripe ran along the top of the fenders and doors.

1967 Surfrider

Pontiac emphasized the ocean influence with a special 1967 GTO convertible called the Surfrider. It was displayed at auto shows with a surfboard resting on the front passenger seat.

The blue interior matched the exterior paint and the unique seat upholstery featured a blue floral-patterned fabric with blue vinyl. The door panels were padded and upholstered up over the window sills unlike other A-bodied Pontiacs of 1967. Armrests on the doors were the longer type with paddle-style door handles (a la 1965-66 Grand Prix/Bonneville).

1967 Skydiver

Pontiac introduced the Firebird in 1967. Almost immediately, a specially trimmed 400 convertible was prepared emphasizing the car's sporty character. It was named the Skydiver for its parachute-like color scheme. It had an exterior finish of orange pearlescent paint with an orange and white matching pearlescent vinyl interior. The carpeting was orange cut pile.

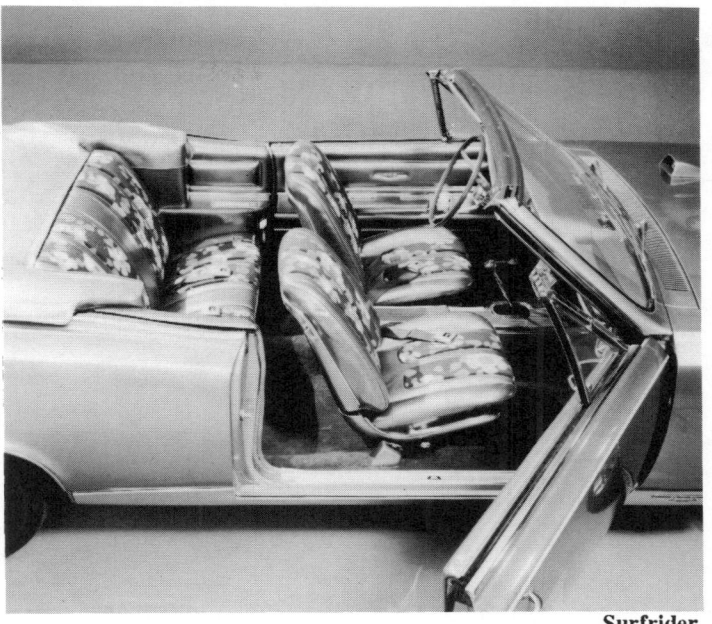

Surfrider

Skydiver

1969 Fiero

1968 Firebird of Tomorrow and 1969 Fiero

The Firebird of Tomorrow was an aerodynamics styling exercise on the 108-inch wheelbase Firebird chassis. The purpose was to exploit fully the advantages of clean unencumbered design. The twin intake grilles and bumper were molded together in Endura rubber. The headlights were hidden behind flush body panels. The door handles were removed and metal nameplates were replaced by decals. The windshield was lowered to reduce frontal area and the pillar posts were eliminated. Behind the cockpit was a combined rollbar-airflow straightener with integrated lateral fins for cross wind stability. All of this, and streamlined sheetmetal 15 inches lower than the production Firebird, provided optimum aerodynamics.

Interesting exterior features included air scoops just ahead of the rear wheels. Their purpose was to cool the rear brakes. At the rear, strip taillights flanked the central exhaust pipe extensions. The exterior was painted tangerine pearlfrost and overall length was 200 inches (12 more than the production Firebird).

The two-passenger interior was upholstered in black vinyl. The car had no console between the bucket seats and the transmission lever and electric clock were mounted on the floor. Six gauges were mounted in the center section of the dash where the air conditioning vent and controls were normally located on production models. The car was powered by a 400 V-8 engine with a 4-speed transmission.

The Firebird Fiero that was displayed at 1969 auto shows was, in fact, the "Firebird of Tomorrow" shown in 1968. Originally shown at the New York Auto Show in the spring of 1968, it was renamed the Firebird Fiero for the 1969 show circuit. The car was painted white with a bold, orange stripe. If surviving photos are reliable, full disc wheel covers were also used on the 1969 version (which also happens to be our main cover car).

1968 Firebird of Tomorrow

1968 Firebird of Tomorrow

1969 Trans Am

The 1969 Trans Am was the ultimate Firebird 400 package, similar in concept to the previously introduced GTO Judge. The Judge was the main push, the Trans Am more or less an easy-to-do after-thought. The basic concept was to combine the hottest engine available with wild visual graphics for the body. In the Trans Am's case, the engine choices were the Ram-Air or the Ram- Air IV 400 cubic inch engines. The graphics were basically America's racing colors, white with blue identification. Twin stripes on the hood, roof and trunk were blue, as were the Trans Am identification decals for the front fenders. There were dual air extractors for the front fenders, an aero wing for the trunk lid and unique hood scoops up front. The Trans Am was a mid-year offering bowing in the spring of 1969. Only 697 cars were built that first year. This year was the last year of the first generation Firebird and a convertible was still being built at the time. Only 8 of those 697 Trans Ams were convertibles.

1969 Firebird 455 HO

The Firebird 400 was the hottest regular production Firebird in 1969, however, one 455 HO Firebird was built. It was an experimental car put together by Jim Aitken and John Sawruk, both Pontiac experimental engine engineers at the time. The engine featured Ram-Air IV heads, exhaust manifolds and valve train, combined with a Tri-Power intake manifold. The exhaust featured the "Tiger Button" which adjusted the sound level. Four exhaust pipes were used with this system. The car was an orange hardtop with the Trans Am spoiler and 455 markings on the hood scoops. The Firebird 455 HO arrived in dealer showrooms for 1971 without the Tri-Power carburetion or the "Tiger Button" exhaust.

1969 GTO Judge

The Judge was a special edition GTO introduced for 1969. It came in hardtop and convertible body styles and featured the 366 hp Ram-Air 400 engine or the optional 370 hp Ram-Air IV engine. Both had driver-controlled air intake scoops. The two less powerful GTO engines for 1969 were not available with the Judge. The suspension was upgraded over the standard GTO and heavy duty springs and shocks were included. Also on the Judge were the 70 series "wide oval" tires.

Styling was altered to give a bolder functional appearance. Initial cars were all painted a Firebird color, Carousel Red. This color, not available on other GTOs, was actually an orange. It made the car stand out anywhere. Later production Judges were available in any GTO color. To accent the bold color, a slash stripe was applied along the top of the front fenders and doors. Pre-production models, illustrated in the catalogue, show this stripe in white. By the time the car hit dealer showrooms in January, the stripe was changed to a blue-red-yellow design. It was also extended under the rear quarter windows. "The Judge" lettering was changed at the same time. Pre-production design used small block letters mounted on the top of the doors just behind the white stripe. It also featured small yellow lettering and a gavel on the right side of the trunk lid. Actual production cars used larger psychedelic blue-red-yellow lettering mounted on the front fenders and the rear airfoil. This exclusive five-foot-wide airfoil was mounted on the trunk lid and the front end featured an exclusive blacked out grille. Rally II wheels were included in the specifications, but without the chrome trim rings.

The Judge was never intended as a high-volume model. Nevertheless, 6,833 were produced in 1969. Only 108 of these were convertibles; the balance were hardtops.

1970 GTO Judge

The Judge returned for a second session in 1970. The sheetmetal was new below the beltline and the most prominent restyling feature was the addition of horizontal ridges above each wheelwell. The tri-color striping was altered to two separate accents above these ridges. "The Judge" lettering was moved to just behind the front wheelwells and onto the rear deck lid. The airfoil featured a more suspended look as the two ends no longer curved to meet the fenders. The front featured the restyled Endura bumper separating the headlamps from the grille cavities. The restyled grille still featured the blacked out effect and the mechanical aspects of the 1970 model were unchanged from 1969. Only 3,797 units were built of which a mere 168 were convertibles.

1971 GTO Judge

The Judge held court for the last time in 1971. The front end styling was redesigned featuring a protruding grille. A new hood design sported wider scoops mounted forward on the hood which improved the air induction system. The rear was left unchanged. White letter tires were now included in the standard specifications. Rally II wheels were still standard, but the new Honeycomb wheels were optional. They featured a urethane surface bonded to a steel wheel giving an alloy appearance. The 455 HO engine was the only powerplant offered in 1971. The 1971 Judge is by far the rarest as only 374 were built. Of these, a paltry 17 were convertibles.

1969 Judge

1970 Judge

1971 Judge

Following pages, 1969 Judge

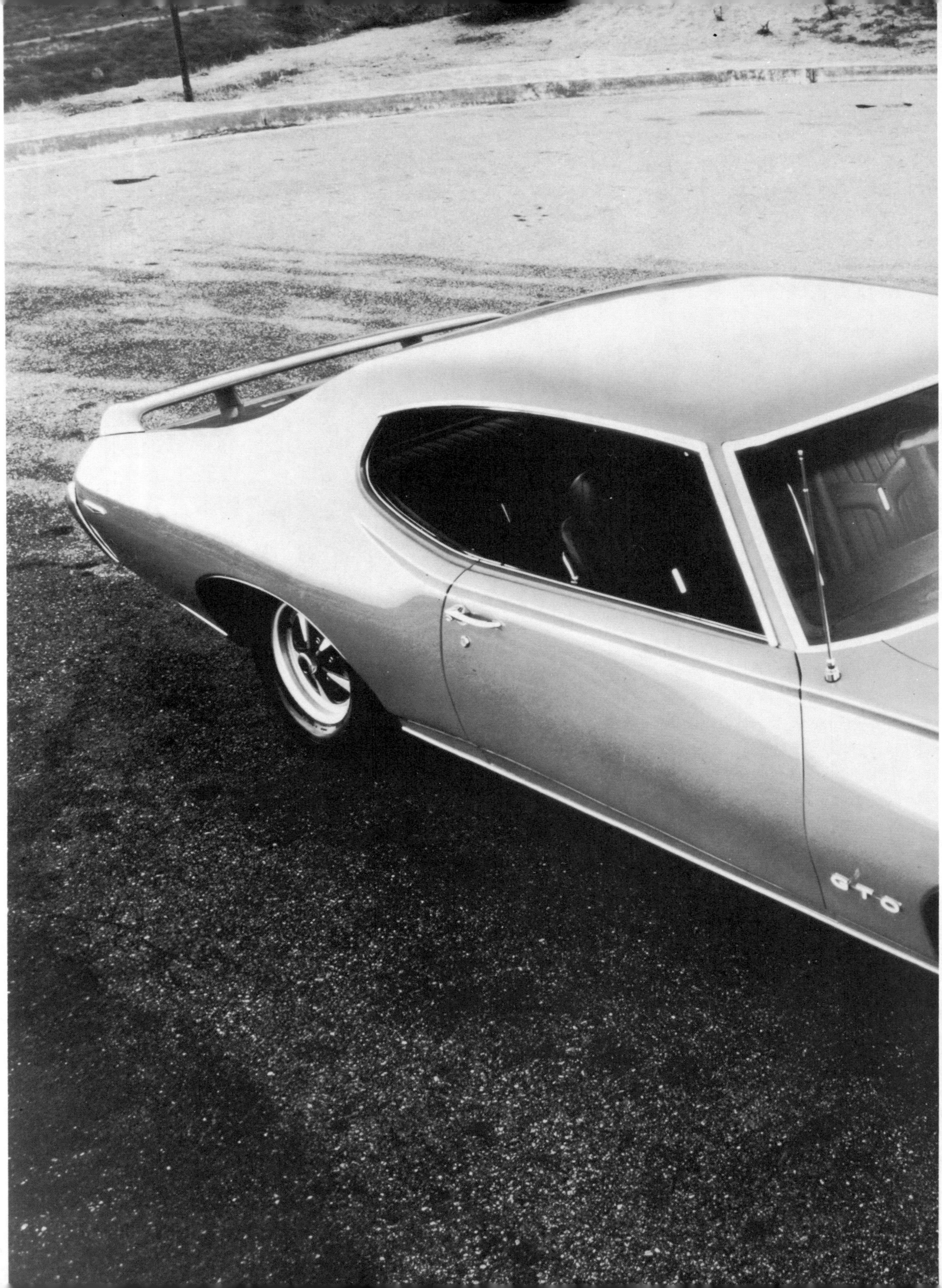
GTO

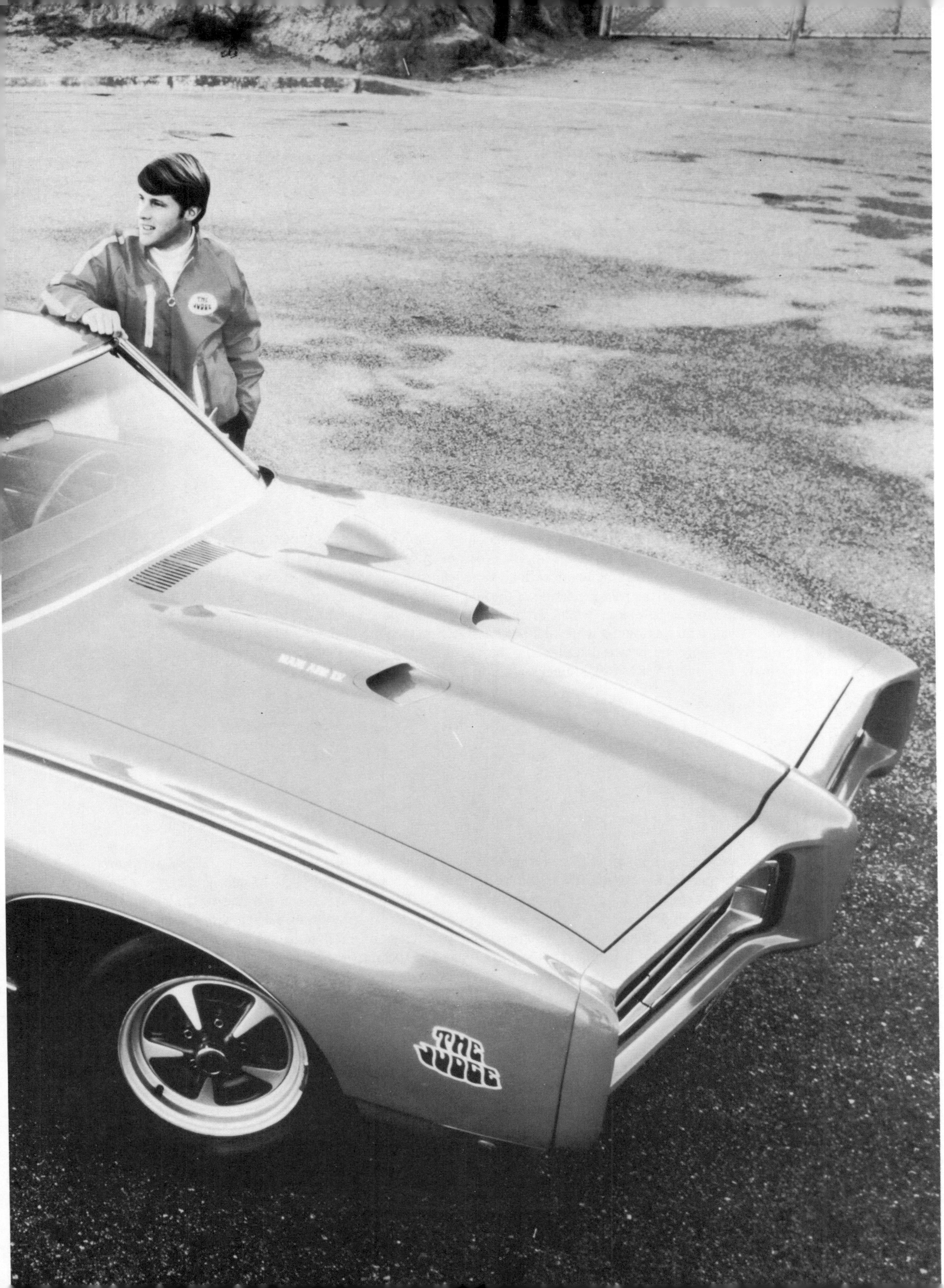
THE JUDGE

1969 E.T. (Elapsed Time) E.T.

The E.T. (Elapsed Time), its proposed name for production, was built in 1969 as a prototype in response to the highly successful Road Runner concept. It was a Tempest two-door sedan with the 350 HO engine and GTO suspension. The engine featured cold air induction with air supplied from a scoop, designed to match the hood tachometer on the driver's side, on the passenger side of the hood. The visuals were surprisingly similar to the GTO Judge. It was painted Firebird Carousel Red (actually more of an orange in appearance) and featured a blacked out grille, Rally II wheels sans trim rings and a white and black stripe along the top of the front fenders and doors--just like the Judge prototype. This concept was distorted into the highline 1969 Judge, then finally reached production in more or less original form in mid-year 1970, although not as the E.T. It was renamed the GT-37.

1970 GT-37

Pontiac's answer to the Plymouth Road Runner arrived in the spring of 1970. Named the GT-37, it featured low-bucks performance. In concept, it was similar to the E.T. experimental of 1969. In sales terms, it was option code 332 for basic Tempest coupes and hardtop coupes with either the 350 two-barrel or the 400 four-barrel engines. The $198 package included G-70 x 14 white letter tires, heavy duty 3-speed transmission with Hurst shifter, Rally II wheels without trim rings, dual exhausts with quad tailpipe extensions through the valance panel (a la GTO), hood locking pins, a side body stripe identical to the 1969 Judge and specific identification on the front fenders and trunk. Only 1,419 GT-37s were built in 1970. Interestingly, Pontiac planning documents indicate that the GT-37 was intended as a lighter-weight, higher-performance car than the GTO.

1971 GT-37

The GT-37 encored for 1971. Although the pillared coupe was still listed in the catalogue, all 1971 GT-37s were hardtop coupes. This was because the vent windows that came with the pillared coupes could not be fully opened with the new body-colored sport mirrors. Early 1971 models featured Judge-like "eyebrow" stripes above each wheelwell and later production models used a full length stripe that was similar to that used on 1972 intermediates. Engine choices were increased to all V-8s from the 350 two-barrel to the 455 HO. Production climbed to 5,802 units for 1971.

1970 GT-37

1971 GT-37 (Owner, John Sawruk)

1969 Steam-Powered Grand Prix

GM Research Laboratories built one experimental steam-powered Grand Prix for 1969. It was the first steam-powered car with complete power accessories and air conditioning. It was strictly an engineering exercise and showed very little consumer appeal. The car weighed 450 lbs more than a conventional Grand Prix, yet had only half the horsepower with a 30-45 second warmup wait. The only appearance change was the grillework around the headlights. This car still belongs to GM.

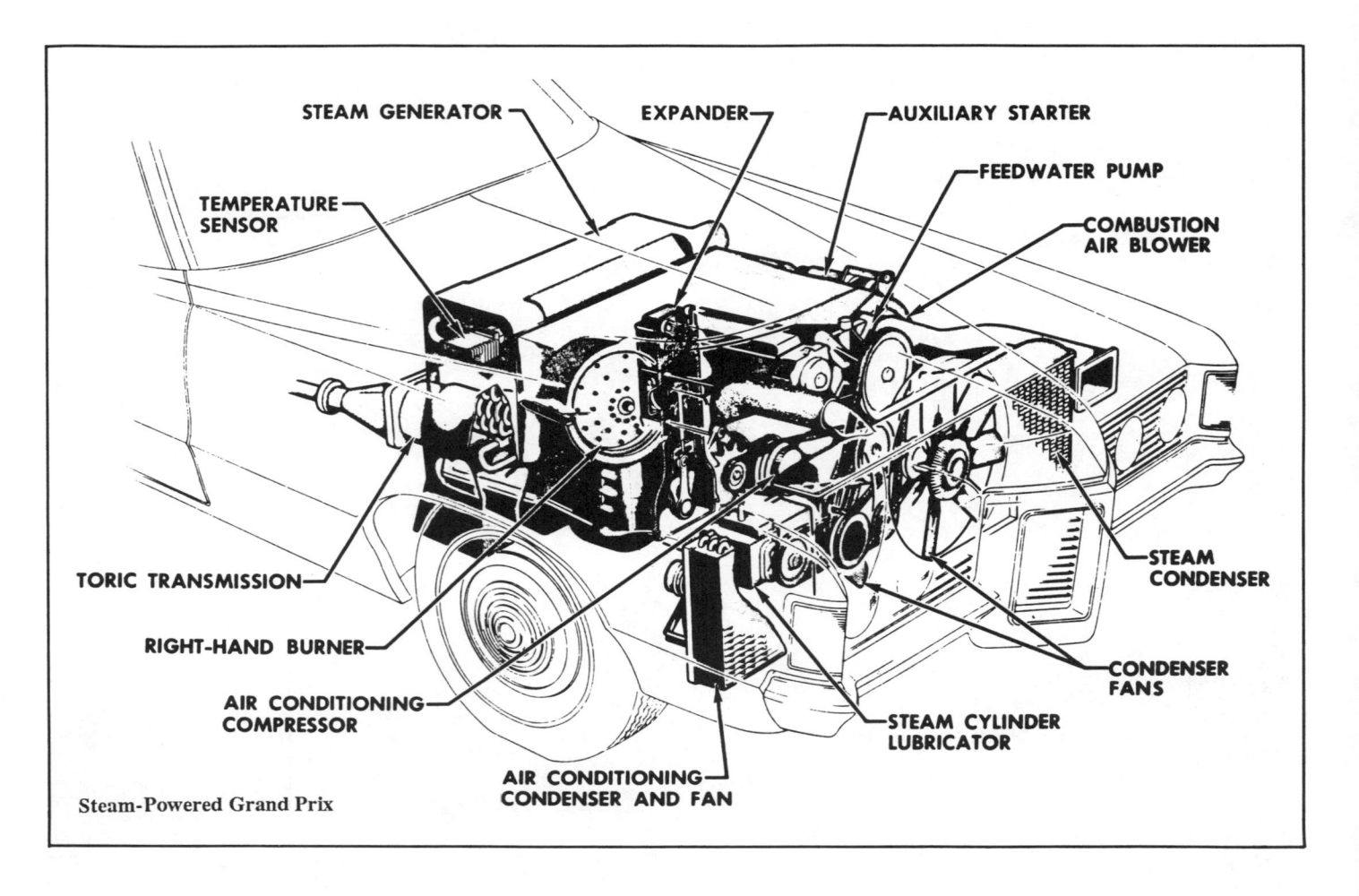

Steam-Powered Grand Prix

1969 Cirrus

Named after a stratospheric cloud formation, the futuristic Cirrus incorporated many airplane features. The two-passenger cockpit featured aircraft-type steering controls consisting of hand grips with thumb buttons to activate the horn and turn signals. The instrument panel and overhead roof console were fitted with instruments, 31 indicator lights, 29 toggle switches and 4 control levers. Entrance to the cockpit was from the rear with passengers moving between the seats as in an airplane. This eliminated the traditional side doors and allowed a single piece of glass to curve around both sides and the front.

The aerodynamic shape was obviously inspired by aircraft design. The undercarriage was completely enclosed and air braking flaps flipped out from each rear side quarter. The car was painted silver with the top surface of the hood and instrument panel a nonreflecting black.

Interesting lighting concepts were used at the rear. The turn signal and stop lights, housed in a narrow horseshoe-shaped strip, showed blue as taillights and changed to red when the brakes were applied. As a separate warning system for emergency stops, two large flipper panels opened across the rear to expose intense flashing red lights.

The Cirrus was originally shown to the public in 1969, but was shown in conjunction with 1970 models as well since nothing on the car identified it with any particular model year.

Cielo del Sol

La Vinta

Cirrus

1970 Cielo del Sol

Spanish names were given to Pontiac's special show cars in 1970. A special Grand Prix was built called the Cielo del Sol (sky of sun). Aptly named, the car featured an electrically-operated sunroof. This did not become a regular factory option until a number of years later. A pearlescent champagne color paint was used on the exterior along with a Cordova top. The interior was leather upholstered.

1970 La Vinta

Carrying on the Spanish theme to the 1970 show cars, the special GTO Judge hardtop was named La Vinta (small boat). Painted a pearlescent orbit orange, the car had all of the typical Judge features: rear air foil, front air dam and side stripes. Oddly enough, it also featured Oldsmobile-style Super Stock wheels.

The interior was not stock GTO. The highback front bucket seats and rear bench were upholstered in black patent leather. No console was provided so the 4-speed transmission shifter was mounted on the floor. The door panels used engine-turned metal plates behind the armrests, the material used on early GTOs and later Trans Ams. The newly introduced Formula steering wheel was also utilized. The seat belts were built into the seat with the shoulder harness emanating from the top of each seatback instead of the roof.

1970 Grand SSJ

Hurst modified 272 Grand Prixs for distribution through Pontiac dealers in 1970. They were called SSJs and were built by GM in either black or white, then shipped to Hurst for the conversion. Hurst applied the gold trim and added the electric sunroof, half vinyl top and digital computer. American aluminum wheels and 15-inch BF Goodrich radial tires were also added.

1971 Grand Prix SSJ

Hurst made 157 SSJ Grand Prixs for 1971. Package content remained the same as 1970. All styling and engineering changes were the same as other Grand Prixs.

1972 Grand Prix SSJ

The final year for the Grand Prix SSJ was 1972. Only 60 cars were converted and there were only detail changes over the 1971 model.

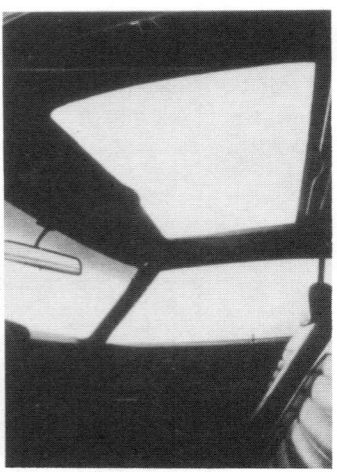

This page, 1970 SSJ

This page, 1971 SSJ

1972 Firebird Pegasus

When the second generation Firebirds were introduced for 1970, they were hailed as looking very much like the exotic Italian sports cars. In 1972, Pontiac stylists took that basic production design one step farther by creating the Pegasus. If ever a Firebird looked like a Ferrari or a Maserati, this one did. The hood was lowered from the fender line and the oval grille protruded from the front of the car. Round parking lights were mounted in the grille cavities and air extractors in the front fenders were louvered. The rear end featured a body-colored bumper and louvered taillamps. Genuine wire wheels with blackwall tires were used. The Pegasus pioneered the wraparound rear window that was introduced on production Firebirds for 1975. It is rumored that this car was equipped with a Ferrari engine.

Edinburgh Grand Prix

1972 Edinburgh Grand Prix

A special show car called the Edinburgh was displayed for 1972. It featured dark paint and upholstery accented with white pinstripes and upholstery piping. Wire wheel styled hubcaps were used on this Grand Prix for a European effect.

1973 Grand Am Station Wagon

A Grand Am station wagon may have been in the plans for the initial 1973 Grand Am series as at least one prototype was built. Like other Grand Ams of that vintage, it was based on the LeMans body and featured a unique Endura front end, pinstriping and exclusive Grand Prix style interior. This prototype also featured the NASA hood with working cold air induction. Initial plans for the 1973 Super-Duty engine included availability in models other than the Trans Am and Formula Firebird. The Grand Am was one of those other applications. This prototype also featured Honeycomb wheels.

Grand Am Wagon

1974 John Player Special Trans Am

The forerunner to the black and gold Special Edition Trans Am of later years was the 1974 Trans Am in John Player Special Colors. The black paint had gold metalflakes and gold pinstripes ran all around the car. The honeycomb polycast wheels were gold colored as well as the recessed headlamp bezels and grille inserts. This combination, sans the gold metalflakes and gold headlight bezels and grille, was used on the 1976 Special Edition Trans Am. Even the unusual English lettering on the front fenders was used later. Oddly enough, the interior color used on this car was light blue.

John Player Special

1974 Catalina Elegante

The Catalina Elegante was a regional offering in 1974. A group of Midwest Pontiac dealers created a special package for the Catalina hardtop coupe to make it look as much like a Lincoln Continental Mark IV as possible. The idea was to copy the Contintental at only a fraction of its price. The Elegante included a full vinyl top with smaller rear quarter windows resembling the popular opera windows of the period. Next to the opera window was an Elegante script nameplate. An exclusive Lincolnesque hood ornament was added atop the grille and incorporated the Pontiac arrowhead emblem in the top portion. The radiator-style grille returned to the Catalina for 1974.

Elegante

1974 Astre Elite

For a year and a half prior to its U.S. introduction in the fall of 1974, the Astre was a Canadian-only Pontiac. It was built and sold only in Canada. For display at the 1974 Toronto Auto Show, GM of Canada prepared a special Astre hatchback featuring a landau vinyl roof with opera windows. Matching the pearlescent white paint, a four-color red stripe with arrows in it was painted on each side. Special wire-type magnesium wheels were used with the red painted hub showing through. The bumper strips were also color-keyed white.

Inside, pearlescent white was carried through in the leather seat upholstery and door panels. "Vera Cruz" cloth, using the four-color red arrow pattern, was used for the insert panels on the seats and doors. Deep pile Trulon plush white carpeting was on the floor.

Astre Elite

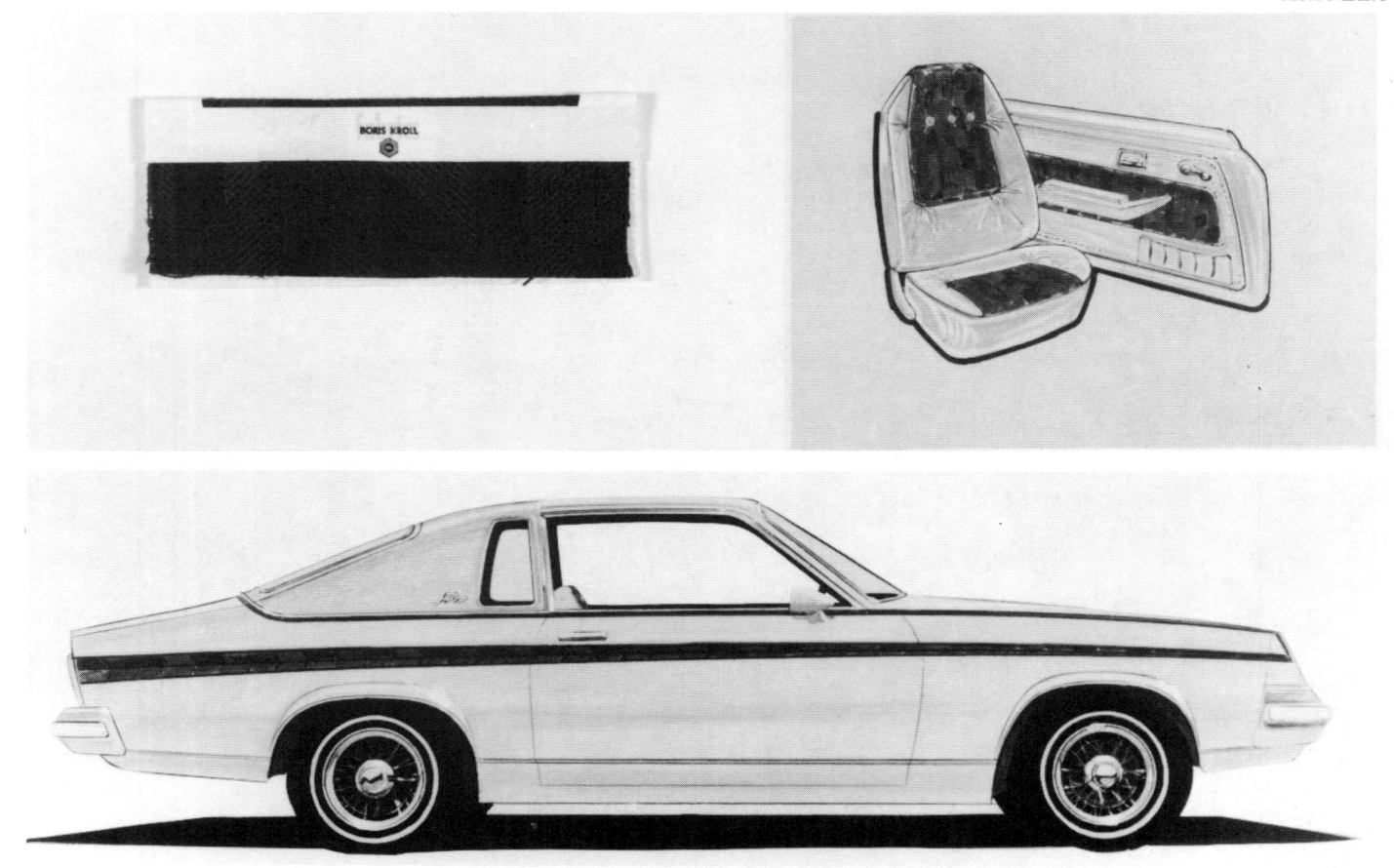

1974 Banshee

Like the original Banshee of 1966, this one, built for 1974, was a Firebird concept car. Developed from the Firebird, it had an all-new exterior and interior. Only the honeycomb wheels and Formula steering wheel and dashboard were from the stock Firebird. Painted a deep metallic red, it was accented with gold pinstripes, wheels, front fender louvers and exhaust pipe extensions. The interior was also red leather with gold accents. Rear seats folded for additional luggage space.

The front was designed for maximum aerodynamics. The bumper utilized a soft face body-colored urethane covering over an energy-absorbing foam base. A six-lamp system of quartz halogen rectangular headlamps were set behind a plastic cover. This system utilized lowbeams, highbeams and special turnpike beams. The hood louvers were a functional ram-air type.

The side glass was fixed and flush with the sheetmetal, again, for increased aerodynamics. An electrically-operated toll window was provided in both doors.

At the rear, the wraparound taillights were recessed in a urethane-covered bumper similar to the front. Signal and stoplights were incorporated into the louvers around the rear windows.

Li'l Wide Track T.M.

1975 Li'l Wide Track

Motortown Corporation of Detroit converted a limited number of Astres to Li'l Wide Tracks in 1975. Both hatchbacks and Safaris were offered through authorized Pontiac dealers. The conversion was entirely cosmetic and designed to give the cars a sportier appearance. The package included special stripes and wheels and a front air dam. The hatchback also included rear quarter window louvers and a rear spoiler.

1975 All-American Grand Am

The All-American Grand Am featured a white exterior with red and blue pinstriping. The "All-American" decals on the trunk lid and rear quarter panels were also red and blue. Even the honeycomb wheels were painted white. Inside, the white seats featured red, white and blue striped inserts with midnight blue carpeting. The car also featured a rear deck spoiler and air deflectors at each wheel. A similar package appeared in 1977 as the Can Am.

1975 Phoenix

The Phoenix was a project in which Pontiac enlisted assistance from the GM Manufacturing Development Staff, several other GM divisions and outside suppliers. The intent was to show weight reduction potentials for automobiles. Some of the design principles learned here were used in GM's downsizing programs that hit showrooms in the 1977 model year.

The project car was a Ventura coupe sans approximately 700 lbs. A smaller and lighter (151 cid, four-cylinder) drivetrain accounted for 300 of those pounds and plastic component design accounted for the rest. Among the plastic features were cast thermoplastic wheels and soft bumpers used in later Firebirds and Grand Ams, but the car also had thermoplastic front fenders. In addition, the car featured a fixed hood with a small service access door on the passenger side for checking engine oil and coolant levels. The car was painted silver-gray with a char- coal gray accent along the rocker panels and lower bumpers. This was set off with red pinstriping and decal lettering. Later Grand Ams and Firebirds also employed this paint scheme.

Phoenix

Phoenix

1976 Special Edition Trans Am

Pontiac built a Special Edition Trans Am for the public following the idea of the John Player Special Trans Am of 1974. It was painted black with special gold striping and had a gold hood bird. The Special Edition featured the new removeable hatchroof panels, although a few were built without the T-top. Only 643 Special Edition Trans Ams were built in 1976.

Trans Am

1976 50th Anniversary Grand Prix

Pontiac celebrated its 50th anniversary in 1976. A commemorative edition Grand Prix was available to the public for the occasion. Exactly 4,807 units were built and were all-gold LJ models with special striping and removeable hatchroof panels. The standup hood ornament and trunk lock cover were of a distinctive anniversary design.

Skybirds, Red Birds and Yellow Birds...

In addition to the celebrates Trans Am "Blackbirds," Pontiac offered several other Firebird "Bird" options. These were all based on the de luxe Esprit line. The all-blue Skybird was announced in mid-1977 and continued over into 1978. In mid-1978, it was replaced by the all-red Redbird option. The Red Bird ran through the end of the 1979 model year. In 1980, a Yellow Bird option made its appearance. There were no similar options in 1981, the final year of the second generation Firebird and the Esprit was not revived when the third generation appeared in 1982.

1978 Firebird Esprit Redbird

1977 Black Special Edition Trans Am

The black and gold Special Edition of 1976 was carried over into 1977 with new front end styling. The new "snowflake" aluminum wheels were added to the package with gold coloring. This was still the only way to get the Trans Am with the hatchroof panels.

Special Edition Trans Am

1977 Phantom

The Phantom was one of Bill Mitchell's last styling exercises before his retirement. Mitchell, head of GM's styling department, long admired the long hood/short deck proportions popular in cars of the thirties. He employed these classic proportions on the Phantom. A Grand Prix chassis was used for the car, although the cockpit was moved even farther back than on a standard Grand Prix. The styling was unique featuring long flowing fenders reminiscent of the Great Gatsby era. There was no radiator grille like that from the thirties, but a more pointed nose in Pontiac style instead. The long hood featured two rows of louvers. The black paint was carried to the wheel covers which featured concentric circles giving the appearance of even larger wheels. The side glass featured only a small portion that opened and there was no running gear in the car as it was strictly a styling exercise. The Phantom was recently donated to the Sloan Museum in Flint, Michigan.

Phantom

1977-79 Trans Am Type K

The first Trans Am Type K was built for the 1977 Chicago Auto Show by the General Motors Design Staff. The Type K (for Kammback) was a specially designed sport wagon based on the Trans Am coupe. The individual rear seatbacks folded down creating a long, flat, carpeted cargo area behind the front seats. Access to this area was through the two gull-wing hatch windows on each side of the car. There was no tailgate as such nor did the rear window open. Black lenses covered the side-to-side rear taillights. These "wall-to-wall" taillights, as well as the two-box rear bumper with central license plate mounting, showed up later on the 1979 Firebird models. The car was painted a unique two-toned silver-gray color scheme with the darker shade used around the bottom edge. The accent pinstriping was gray and red and the Firebird hood decal was gray and blue. The interior was a matching silver-gray.

Public response was so instantaneously favorable that Pontiac executives gave very serious thought to producing such a car. Sergio Pininfarina, the Italian coachbuilder, was commis- sioned to build two more prototype Type Ks for 1978. One was silver with red interior and the other was gold with beige interior. Both had upgraded carpeting. During 1978, the Italian-built models replaced the original car for publicity purposes. Later, they were given the 1979 front end styling to further lengthen their lives as show cars. The gold car has since been destroyed, but the silver version remains in factory hands.

Can Am

1977 Can Am

The 1977 Can Am was a mid-year model designed to put some Trans Am excitement into the poorly-selling LeMans line. It was available strictly as a coupe with the louvered rear quarter windows. The package also included an exclusive rear deck spoiler and Trans Am-type "Shaker" hood scoop. All 1,000+ units built were painted white with black rocker panels and window moldings. Tri-color (red, orange, yellow) striping was used on the hood, doors, rear spoiler, hood scoop and sport mirrors. The identification lettering matched the tri-color stripes. Rally II wheels were painted white and included trim rings. Under the hood was the Trans Am 6.6 engine, a Pontiac-built 400 cubic inch motor. Cars sold in California and high-altitude counties had the Oldsmobile-built 403 engine, the same as other Pontiac models of that year. Turbo Hydramatic was the only transmission offered.

Grand Am CA

1978 Grand Prix SSJ

Pontiac dealers in Indiana and Ohio offered a Grand Prix SSJ in 1978. This was not a Hurst conversion like the earlier SSJs, but rather a dealer-installed appearance package for the new downsized GP. The package included a unique vinyl landau roof with smaller back window and opera windows. The roof also featured an aluminum Targa band in brushed silver or anodized gold. Etched glass SSJ decals were added to the opera windows and a special accent stripe was included for the top of the front fenders and doors. SSJ identification was added to the front fenders, rear deck lid and Targa band.

Grand Prix SSJ

1978 Grand Am CA

Patterned after the 1977 Can Am production car, Pontiac experimented with a CA version of the 1978 Grand Am. Available photographs show what could be three separate cars. The same car, however, may have been photographed in various stages of development. One photo shows essentially a stock car with four nonstock features: Viscount bucket seats, T-bar hatch roof, rear deck spoiler and air deflectors at each wheel. Other photos show it with the above and hood-mounted information center showing elapsed time and rpm, special striping and decal lettering, Trans Am's WS-6 suspension package (15-inch extra wide aluminum wheels and four-wheel disc brakes), and Pirelli 235/60 x 15 blackwall tires. Also at this stage, black matte moldings replaced chrome on window moldings, taillamp bezels and rub strip molding. At this point, the car was shown without a hatch roof. A final show version added a T-bar hatch roof and smoked glass headlight covers and running lights.

1978 Sunbird Sport Coupe Convertible

The special one-off Sunbird Sport Coupe featured a unique roof design. It combined the structural rigidity of a fixed roof coupe with the open-air feeling of a convertible. With this design, the car retained the A, B and C pillars to support the top. In fact, from the side view, the car does not even appear to be a convertible. Unlike a conventional sunroof-equipped car, most of the top was open to the sky when the top was in the open position. The opening even extended partially over the rear seat. The cloth top stowed at the very rear of the roof and the rear window dropped out of sight, further emphasizing the open-air feeling. A recessed rear window cove, fixed louvered rear quarter windows and a rear deck spoiler were other special features of the car.

Sunbird Sport Coupe

1978 Grand Am Sport Truck

GMC Truck and Coach Division introduced a version of the intermediate Chevrolet El Camino in 1971 called the Sprint. It later was renamed the Caballero. All along, it has been a true badge-engineered vehicle as only the nameplates distinguish it from a Chevrolet. It has always puzzled this author why the Sprint or Caballero did not use more Pontiac, Oldsmobile or Buick parts which were certainly available and would have given the vehicle far more distinction. This is especially perplexing since GMC franchises are so often dualled with Pontiac, Olds or Buick (and seldom with Chevrolet).

In 1978, this issue was addressed by Pontiac engineering, who built a Grand Am Sport Truck proposal vehicle. A Caballero was requisitioned, then altered with Grand Am parts including front end sheetmetal, "snowflake" aluminum wheels and complete Pontiac interior including dash, Custom Sport steering wheel, bucket seats, console and door panels. Even a Pontiac 301 V-8 engine was installed. Some exclusive exterior striping was added, as were the Safari vertical strips on the tailgate. The proposal was to produce the Grand Am Sport Truck for Pontiac dealers and a similar vehicle with LeMans trim for GMC truck dealers. It was not pursued by management. The vehicle was later used as a workhorse by Pontiac and received the updated 1980 style Grand Am grillework. It has since been restored as part of Pontiac's historical vehicle collection, retaining the 1980 style front end.

Grand Am Sport Truck

Grand Am Sport Truck

69

1979 Tenth Anniversary Trans Am

1979 10th Anniversary Limited Edition Trans Am

The Pontiac Trans Am was at the peak of its popularity in 1979 as over 117,000 were built in that model year. To celebrate the 10th anniversary of the Trans Am, a special limited edition was offered to the public. Only 7,500 units were manufactured and all were painted platinum silver with charcoal accents. There was a special black-gray-and-red firebird on the hood that served partially as a divider between the silver and charcoal. The hatchroof panels were silver tinted and the leather and vinyl interior was crafted in a special silver color. The 10th Anniversary model also served as the exclusive introduction to the red instrument panel lighting and the turbo cast aluminum wheels. It also had the first use of embroidered emblems on upholstery--in this case, firebirds on the door trim panels. Many Trans Ams options were included in all anniversary editions: air conditioning, AM/FM stereo radio with seek/scan and tape, power windows, power door locks, quartz halogen headlamps, WS6 suspension with four-wheel disc brakes, white letter tires. The 10th Anniversary Trans Am was the pace car for the 21st Daytona 500 race. The actual pace car was a stock 4-speed Pontiac with special high-speed tires and special side lettering.

Two drivetrain choices were offered: the Pontiac-built 400 cubic inch engine with 4-speed transmission or the less-powerful Olds-built 403 cubic inch engine with Turbo Hydramatic. Californians were offered only the Olds-engined automatics.

1978-79 Black & Gold Special Edition Trans Ams

The Special Edition Trans Am continued as a popular option with the revamped front and rear styling in 1978, but the dominant color was changed from black (with gold trim) to gold (with black trim). The removeable hatchroof panels remained as part of the package, although the car was available without if so desired. The color change was not universally popular with Trans Am buffs who had grown quite fond of their "blackbird" editions, and so, in mid-1979, the gold versions was dropped and the blackbird quietly returned to the catalogue.

1979 Gold Special Edition Trans Am

1979 Grand Prix Landau Convertible

Once again, Pontiac used their personal luxury car, the Grand Prix, for a special show model. At a time when special coachbuilders were the only ones producing convertibles on U.S. chassis, Pontiac pulled off one of their own. A unique rollbar-type "B" pillar replaced the "C" pillar completely leaving the area over the rear seat open. Removeable rose-colored hatch roof panels covered the front seats. The net effect of these roof modifications was a "targa" convertible allowing maximum open-air feeling with the security of a fixed roof structure.

The hatch panels were keyed to the color scheme of the rest of the car. Painted a two-toned rose mist and carmine with carmine interior, the interior was completely stock with leather upholstered Viscount bucket seats with center console and custom sport steering wheel. On the exterior, the regular SJ/LJ rocker panel moldings were used along with the wire wheels (not the hubcap type). The taillamps were to be used in 1980 although this was not revealed at the time. Hidden headlamps were utilized for the first time on a Grand Prix since the 1968 model.

1979 Banshee

Originally shown in 1975, then updated for 1977, the Banshee was changed modestly again for 1979. A new rear bumper and taillight assembly changed the appearance of the rear of the car. The new bumper was more aerodynamic than the previous one. It also incorporated twenty small circular taillamps, ten on each side. New rectangular exhaust extensions replaced the previous round ones and new white-lettered Goodyear GT radials replaced the "Steelgards" used in 1977. Finally, aluminum snowflake wheels replaced the honeycombs. Otherwise, the car remained as previously shown.

Banshee

Grand Prix Convertible

Banshee

1980 Sterling Edition Grand Prix

Grand Prix sales were sagging badly by mid-year 1980. To spark some life into the line, a limited number of Sterling Edition Grand Prixs were built in the spring. They featured a unique two-tone paint job. The lower color (charcoal, a Firebird color) was used only in the rocker panels and around the wheel openings. The rest of the car was silver. Actually, this was just the bottom part of the "double two-tone paint" offered that year. The interior featured LJ style bench seats in a unique black and gray combination not available elsewhere. Special tape inserts on the door handles proclaimed "Sterling Edition".

Sterling Edition Grand Prix

1979 Bonneville Sport Coupe

Pontiac returned the bucket seats and console options to the Bonneville coupe in 1979 after an absence of 10 years. In commemoration, a specially trimmed car was prepared for display. This Bonneville Sport Coupe was white with lower side panels painted gold. The striping was gold and black and window frame moldings and grille insets were painted black. The rear fender skirts and wheel opening moldings were omitted lending a sportier flavor to the car.

Bonneville Sport Coupe

1980 Trans Am Limited Edition Indy 500 Pace Car

About 5,700 Indianapolis 500 Pace Car Limited Edition Trans Ams were built for 1980, all with the new turbocharged 301 cubic inch Pontiac V-8. The car was not offered in California where the Pontiac engines were not certified in 1980. All California Trans Ams were Chevy 305s in that year. No pace cars were built with the Chevy engines and, consequently, none were sold in California.

The exterior paint scheme was similar to that of the 1979 10th Anniversary Trans Am except that white replaced silver. Charcoal was still used as an accent and the firebird on the hood was still black, gray and red. The turbo cast aluminum wheels and the headlamp bezels were painted white, the interior featured oyster-colored vinyl buckets with hobnail cloth inserts and embroidered birds were added to the door pads and the center of the rear seat. The Formula steering wheel was wrapped in genuine leather. The silver tinted hatchroof panels and red instrument panel were carried over from the 1979 Limited Edition. Many of the Trans Am options were included in the pace car model: air conditioning, AM/FM stereo with seek/scan and cassette, power windows and WS6 suspension. The actual pace car was altered only slightly from the ones available to the public in that high-speed tires were added, the air conditioning was removed and the rear axle ratio was changed from 2.56:1 to 3.08:1.

Trans Am Pace Car

1981 Americana Special Edition Grand Prix

The 1981 Americana Special Edition Grand Prix was a special regional model offered by Pontiac dealers primarily in the East. This special edition amounted to little more than a special roof option created by Evans Automotive. It featured a landau top with small opera windows and a metal Targa band trim piece over the roof.

Americana Grand Prix

1980-81 Black Special Edition Trans Am

The Black Special Edition Trans Am continued for 1980. The only change was the availability of the turbo cast aluminum wheels for turbocharged, WS6 suspension cars. The second generation Firebird was in its last year in 1981. The popular black special edition continued little-changed to the end.

1980-81 Black Special Edition Trans Am

75

1981 NASCAR Pace Car

1981 NASCAR Pace Car

A Firebird Trans Am was used to pace the Daytona 500 again in 1981. The white pace car is illustrated above. Note the unusual white wheels. No pace cars were offered for sale to the public.

1981 LeMans GT

This special edition Pontiac was produced for the Canadian market only. Powered by a 267 cid V8, the LeMans GT featured special black-and-gold or maroon-and-gold paint, replete with striping and maple leaf emblems (the latter to increase its Canadian identification). Much of the usual LeMans trim was blacked out on the GT and the performance suspension was a mandatory option. It was announced in the spring of 1981 as a mid-year model and a total of 477 were reportedly built. Clyde Foster, of Toronto, owns the one of these rare cars shown here.

1981 LeMans GT

1982 Recaro Trans Am

The closest Pontiac came to a 1982 Special Edition Trans Am was with the Recaro Trans Am. It featured the black and gold color combination offered previously, but then all black Trans Ams for 1982 used gold trim. The Recaro seats were the focal point of the car, but the limited edition package also included the removeable hatchroof panels and the WS6 suspension package (similar to previous years). About 2,000 Trans Ams were built in 1982 with the Recaro package.

1982 Trans Am NASCAR Pace Car

Pontiac traditionally paces the Daytona 500 race. The pace car for 1982 was a red Trans Am. Similar cars paced the races at Talladega, Charlotte, Rockingham, Darlington, North Wilkesboro, Martinsville and Bristol. No pace car replicas were offered to the public in 1982.

1983 25th Anniversary Daytona 500 Limited Edition Trans Am

Pontiac's series of limited and special edition Trans Ams continued for 1983 with the 25th Anniversary Daytona 500 Limited Edition Trans Am. The Daytona 500 is probably the best known of America's stock car races and to celebrate its 25th anniversary, Pontiac created a distinctive pace car and offered 2,500 replicas to the public. It featured a mid-body two-toned color combination of white upper with gray

NASCAR Pace Car

metallic lower and white aluminum wheels. This special edition Trans Am was the first to offer the aero package including front air dam, grille pads and side rocker fences. These became regular production options in 1984 and standard equipment in 1985. The interior featured Recaro seats with leather and suede upholstery and red instrument panel lighting. Also included in the package were the WS6 suspension package and AM/FM stereo with cassette and graphic equalizer.

25th Anniversary Daytona Trans Am

1983 Pikes Peak Pace Car

1983 Pikes Peak Pace Car

A white turbo Sunbird was selected at the official Pace Car of the 1983 Pikes Peak event. This was the first use of the turbo four-cylinder engine. No pace car replicas were offered for sale to the public, however.

1983 2000 Sunbird

Pontiac catalogued a convertible in 1983 after a seven-year absence. The last ragtop was the 1975 Grand Ville produced totally in house. For 1983, a 2000 Sunbird convertible was offered by sending specially prepared coupes to American Sunroof Company for conversion. This was only the third time in Pontiac's history that the division sought outside help for bodywork on low production models. The first time was from 1927-1932 when Stewart bodies were used on open cars, although the cars were assembled at Pontiac's factory. The second time was in the wood-bodied station wagon era from 1937-1948, when Her- cules and Ionia built the wood bodies on Pontiac chassis.

The 2000 Sunbird was originally shown to the press in the summer of 1982 and to the public in the 1983 catalogue issued in the fall of 1982. The cars, however, were not available until spring, 1983, and then in strictly limited quantities. Only 626 were built in that initial year. Production increased markedly in subsequent years when the 2000 nameplate was dropped. ASC continued to perform the conversion.

2000 Sunbird

1983 Firebird 500

1983 Firebird 500 Limited Edition

Five hundred copies of a limited edition Firebird were made for the Southern California market in 1983. All featured silver/gray paint with a full-length side body stripe. Also featured were a unique black rear deck spoiler and special Firebird 500 Limited Edition decal for the roof sail panel. Certain regular production options were included with car as well: 5 liter V-8 engine, custom interior, AM/FM stereo with cassette. Inside, there was a serialized dash plaque mounted above the radio.

1984 Firebird 500

1984 Firebird 500 LE

For 1984, Pontiac, again, offered a limited edition Firebird for Southern California. It was dubbed the Firebird 500 LE (Limited Edition) as only 500 copies were built. It was similar in content to the 1983 version employing the 5 liter V-8 engine, custom interior, AM/FM stereo with cassette and serialized dash plaque. All 1984 models were painted white with blue stripes and blue interiors. Even the rear spoiler was painted white. The stripes were relocated to a lower position and wrapped around the entire vehicle. The 500 LE designation was incorporated into the stripes and, on first glance, the car had a similar appearance to the 15th Anniversary Trans Am.

1984 MVP Trans Am

In conjunction with "Sport" magazine, Pontiac began awarding a new Trans Am to the most valuable players in the sports world. The first to receive such a car was Super Bowl XVI MVP Joe Montana. MVP cars have also been awarded to the NHL Stanley Cup Championship MVP, the NBA Championship MVP and the World Series MVP. When the eighth car of the series was awarded to Super Bowl XVIII MVP Marcus Allen, Pontiac created a special promotion for its dealers. A set of "MVP Most Valuable Player" decals for the Trans Am doors were made available to match those of the car given away. The decals could be applied to any Trans Am in the dealer's stock as long as it was red with black aero package and charcoal interior. This was the color combination of Marcus Allen's car. Quantities were not limited as dealers could order as many as they wished. The decals were designed as a permanent part of the car. Offered separately, were a set of temporary decals dealers could put on a showroom car and remove at a later date.

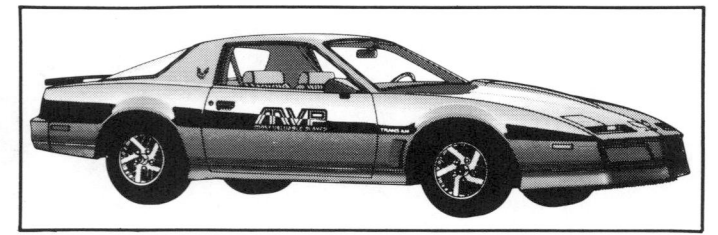

MVP Trans Am

MVP Trans Am

Fiero Pace Car

Fiero Pace Car

Fiero Pace Car

1984 Fiero Indy Pace Car

Pontiac paced the 1984 Indianapolis 500 with their new Fiero. The car featured a 2.7 liter, Super-Duty, four-cylinder engine with over-the-counter parts. The engine developed 232 hp at 6500 rpm and was not directly available from the factory. The car also featured a nonstock air intake snorkle above the roof, built-in yellow strobe lights and chrome 16-inch wheels with 50 series tires. There were actually three cars built to these specifications and featured a redesigned front end and rocker fences along the side. These styling elements showed up later on the 1985 Fiero GT.

A unique white with gray accents paint combination was employed and the interior featured slate gray leather seats with red cloth inserts. The red and gray were used on exterior graphics as well. About 2,000 replica pace cars were offered to the public just before the race. These did not have the Super-Duty engine, air snorkle or 16-inch wheels with 50 series tires. They did, however, feature an engine appearance package on the standard four-cylinder which included red spark plug wires, silver painted rocker cover, painted air cleaner, stainless steel oil filler cap and dual outlet exhaust system with dual extensions per side. The interior and exterior details of the pace car were reproduced in the replicas.

Pikes Peak Fiero

1984 Fiero Pikes Peak Auto Hill Climb Pace Car

One Fiero Indy Pace Car replica was used as a pace car for the 1984 Pikes Peak Hill Climb in July, 1984.

1984 Fiero Space Frame Demonstration Exhibit

To demonstrate the significance of the Fiero's space frame chassis, a special auto show exhibit was prepared where three identical triplet girls snapped the Enduraflex exterior panels of the car on and off. With the panels off, the driveable chassis could be viewed by the public. When the exterior panels were put back on, the car looked like any other red Fiero.

Space Frame Fiero

Fiero SD4

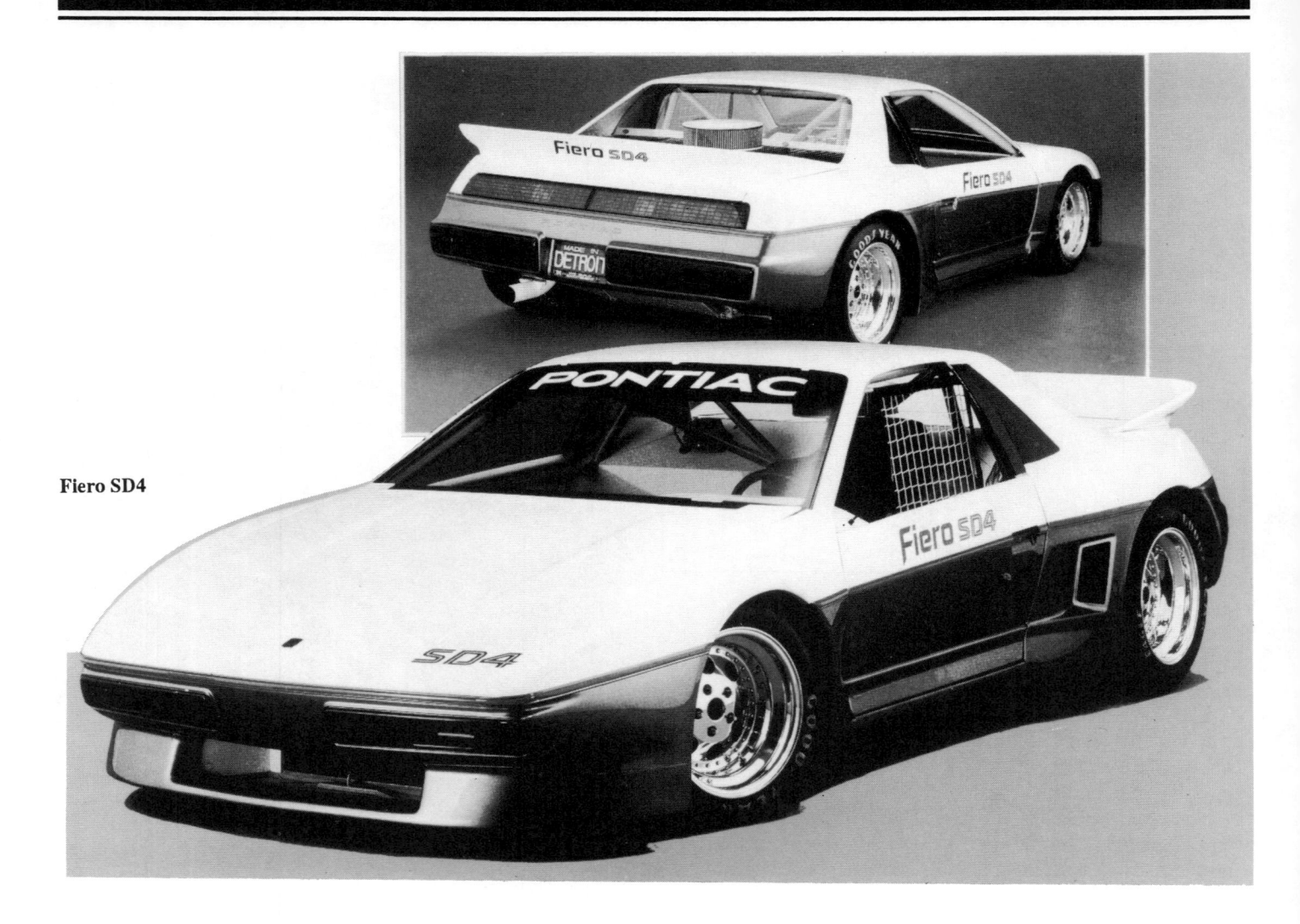

1984 Fiero SD4

The Fiero SD4 was an IMSA racer developed for the auto show circuit to display aftermarket products available for the Fiero. It featured a mid-body, two-toned paint scheme in white upper with grey-brown lower. It was shown at Fiero introduction time.

1984 Fiero GTS Spyder/Roadster

Almost from the day of its introduction, people have been speculating on an open-roofed Fiero. The GTS Spyder/Roadster was shown as a Fiero roadster prototype as early as the East and West Coast long lead press previews in June, 1983. It was not a convertible, as it had no folding fabric top. A molded fiberglass panel was mounted around the headrests behind the Recaro seats. The roadster was originally gold, but later updated with a yellow-gold paint job, and, still later, with a two-tone gold paint scheme and gold high-tech wheels. At that time, the aero package from the Indy pace car was added. The roadster also featured an air scoop on both rear fenders. This car is currently a part of the Pontiac historical vehicle collection.

1985 Fiero Convertible

A genuine Fiero convertible was built in 1985 with a folding fabric top. The rear deck panel was changed on this car so that it was hinged on the driver's side and opened to the passenger side. The convertible top was stowed amazingly in the small space behind the seats. The convertible previewed the 1986 Fiero GT rear end styling. It was

Fiero GTS Spyder

Fiero GTS Spyder

Following pages, Fiero Convertible

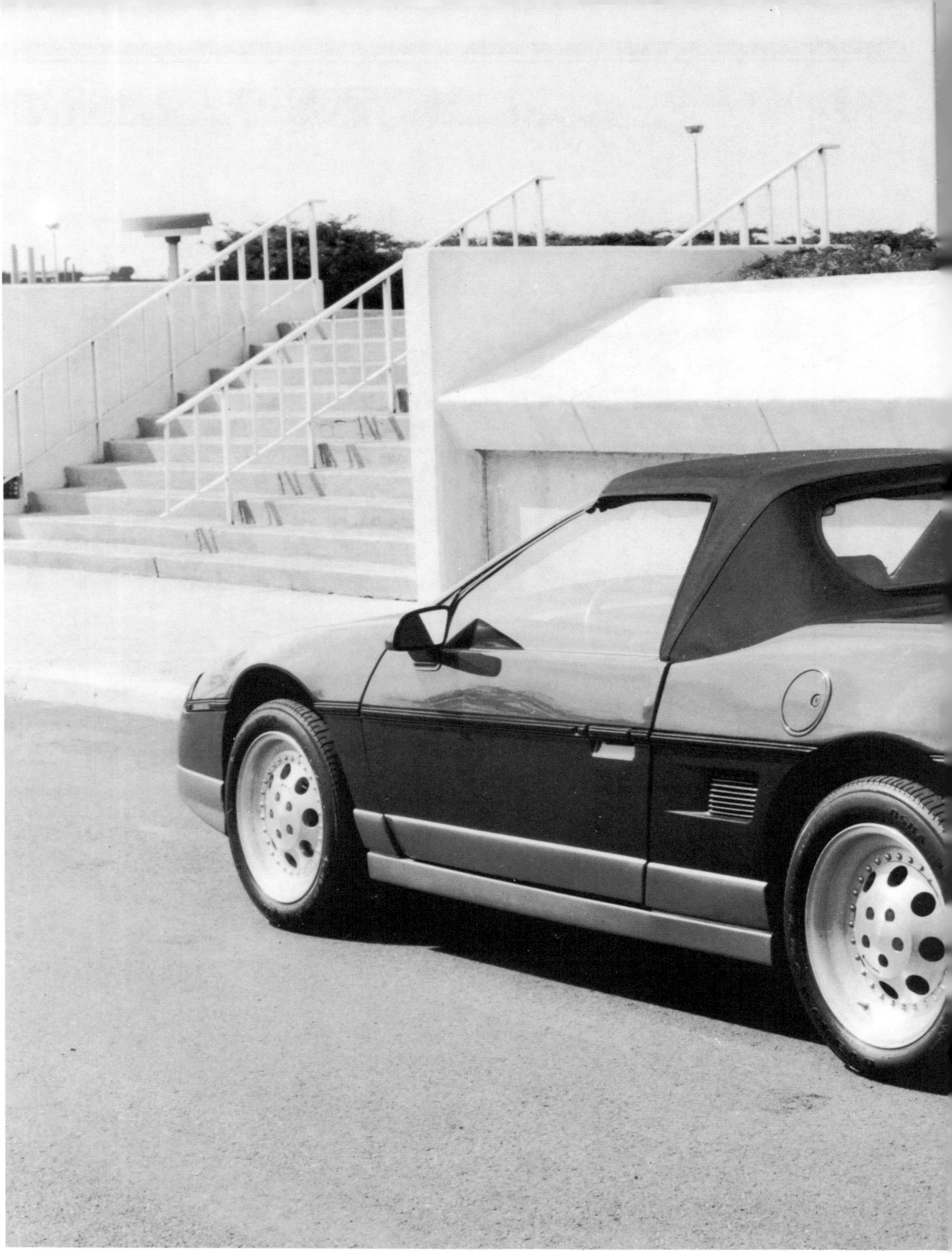

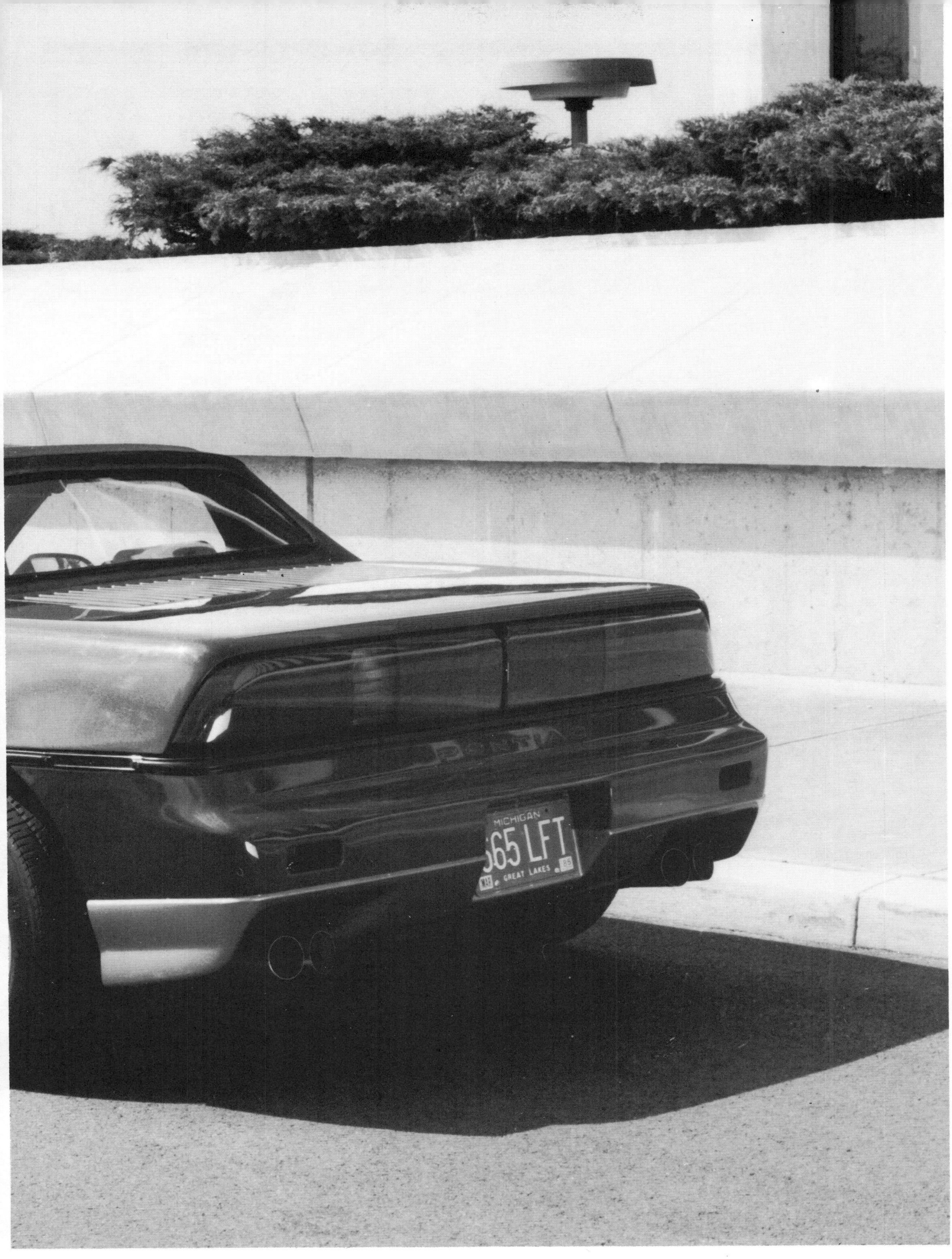
MICHIGAN
65 LFT
GREAT LAKES

Fiero Convertible

1984 Car Craft Fiero

"Car Craft" magazine was doing quite a bit of work with Pontiac Motor Division in developing special Fiero applications. One of the results was this 1985 Car Craft Fiero. It used a Super-Duty four-cylinder engine for guts and special graphics to drive the point home. It was featured on the pages of "Car Craft" magazine. This car is currently in the Pontiac historical vehicle collection.

Fiero by Car Craft

Fiero Four-Seater

Fiero Four-Seater

So exciting was the new Fiero that everyone, it seemed, got into the act of modifying, improving or hotting up the new mid-engine car. Not content to let GM Design have the last corporate word, Pontiac developed this four-seater Fiero 2+2 on its own. It looked pretty good from the angle in the photo reproduced here, less so (alas) from other angles. Still, it was an intriguing concept car. The main purpose was to demonstrate the applicability of the space frame technology for larger vehicles.

1984 15th Anniversary Trans Am

The Trans Am celebrated its 15th anniversary in 1984 with a limited edition anniversary model. The original 1969 color combination of white with blue graphics was used on all cars. The aero package was white to match the main body color. Other Trans Ams used a two-color combination. The monochromatic combination became a regular production option in 1985. The large Trans Am lettering on the side was exclusive to this model, as were the white taillight louvers. By far the most distinguishing feature of the car was the new 16-inch wheels with 50 series tires. In 1984, this was the only F-car with these wheels. Other Trans Ams and Camaros got them in 1985.

The interior featured Recaro seats in Light Sand Gray leather with Medium Sand Gray cloth inserts. The package also included the HO engine, WS6 suspension and removeable hatchroof panels.

1985 Trans Am Kammback

1985-86 Trans Am Kammback

The Firebird Kammback, actually a Trans Am, continued the wagon concept of the 1977 Type K exercise. The Type K wagon on the second generation Firebird body proved to be too costly for production. The current Firebird body is already built as a hatchback, making it far simpler to produce a wagon style. In this case, the hatchback panel was simply replaced with one with a squared-off kammback style. In this one-off styling exercise, the rear was bolted closed. The car was built to test the feasibility of its addition to the production schedule. This particular car was a blue and silver Trans Am with WS6 suspension.

As we go to press, a second, 1986 Kammback has been completed. The new version is bright red with a saddle interior and bears "GTA" identification on the exterior. No plans exist to put it into productionat this date.

1986 Trans Am GTA Kammback

1985 Sunbird SE Pace Car

Pontiac paced the Pikes Peak Hill Climb again in 1985. This time, a Sunbird SE hatchback was used with the turbo motor. No replicas were offered by Pontiac dealers.

Sunbird Pace Car

1985 GTO

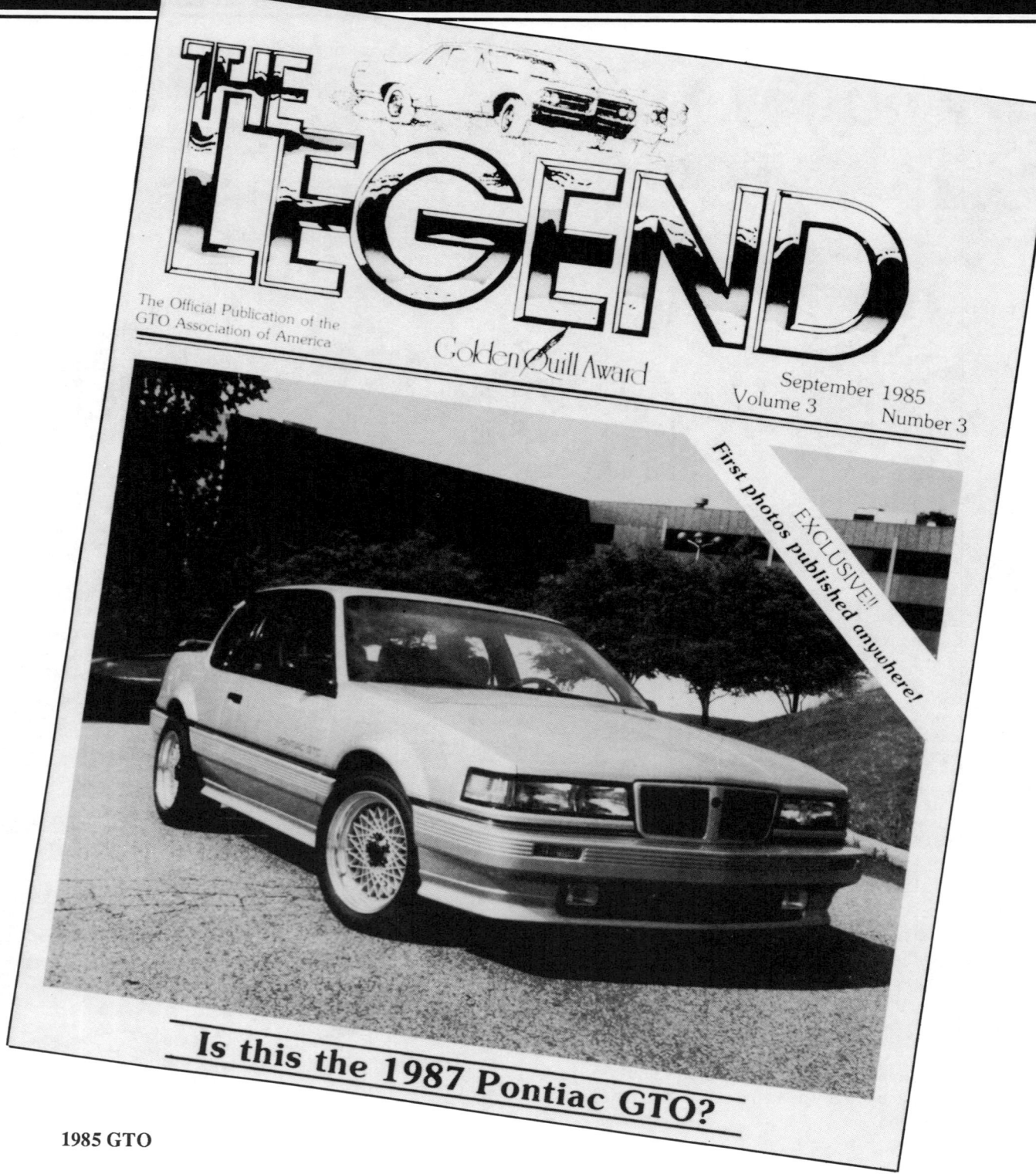

The GTO nameplate returned in 1985 on one of Pontiac's engineering exercises. The GTO was based on the highly successful Grand Am coupe. It was painted silver with a blacked out grille and black and red accents. The car featured flush headlamps, air dam and side rocker extensions that showed up in 1986 on the Grand Am SE. It also featured a trunk-mounted airfoil and a Super-Duty 2.7 liter, four-cylinder with 16-valve head developing 230 hp. Due to the large amount of horsepower, the engine was mated to a Turbo Hydramatic transmission. The Y99 suspension was modified with four-wheel disc brakes, 16-inch wheels and 50 series tires. The interior included a four-spoke Momo steering wheel and four bucket seats (of which the rear pair were removable).

The GTO Association of America scooped the industry in reporting this model as its cover car with the September, 1985, issue of the club publication. The front cover is reproduced here. (P.S. No, this GTO prototype was not scheduled for 1987 introduction! Much of the exterior add-ons did, however, appear on the 1986 Grand Am SE.)

Trans Sport Interior

1986 Trans Sport

Pontiac created a unique multipurpose concept vehicle for 1986 named the Trans Sport. The vehicle was totally new from the ground up with an exceptionally rounded and aerodynamic body. There was generous use of glass in the steeply raked windshield and side glass that curved over the roofline. A gull-wing door was used for the right rear entrance.

Inside were six fully articulating individual seats with individual radio controls and headphones for each. A rear-mounted television and laser disc player were also found. A personal computer on the passenger side of the dash pro- vided information on weather, traffic, navigation and travel assistance. The front-wheel-drive Trans Sport was powered by a 2.9 liter, turbocharged, aluminum V-6 engine with automatic transmission. The transmission was controlled electrically from the driver's armrest.

1986 2+2

Pontiac revived an old nameplate in 1986 with the introduction of the 2+2. This nomenclature was used on sporty Catalinas from 1964 through 1967 and, in Canada, on Parisiennes from 1967 through 1970. A Grand Prix version bowed for 1986. As in earlier times, it denoted a sporty version of a standard car line. The 1986 2+2 featured a 165 hp, 305 V-8 engine, 4-speed Turbo Hydramatic transmission, limited slip differential, 15-inch Rally II wheels with Eagle GT tires and gas-filled shocks. The exterior featured a unique two-toned combination of silver upper and medium gray lower with red accent striping. The traditional Grand Prix radiator grille was replaced by an aerodynamic soft fascia panel with four grille cavities. The rear end was characterized by a fiberglass deck lid with spoiler and a large sweeping rear window. The aerodynamic front and rear characteristics were designed to enhance the car's stock car racing drag coefficient. The 2+2 was a no-option car; everything was standard equipment.

The idea had been first proposed by Richard Petty Enterprises in 1983. They went so far as to produce a prototype with a soft, aerodynamic fascia not unlike the ultimate 1986 2+2.

2+2 Interior

1983 Richard Petty Grand Prix prototype

Great American Race Pace Car

1986 Great American Race Pace Cars

Twenty white Trans Ams were selected to pace the 4th Annual Interstate Batteries Great American Race, run from June 25th to July 5th 1986. The Great American Race is a "controlled speed" event, i.e., a rally, that caters to pre-1937 vehicles. The 1986 race kicked-off at Disneyland, in Anaheim, California, and wended its way to the Statue of Liberty Centennial Celebration in New York City. In between lay a 3,500 mile route through 14 states that took 11 days to complete. The pace cars were stock, white Trans Ams featuring Great American Race decals.

Fiero GTP

As we go to press, Pontiac has just announced the Fiero GTP IMSA racing car. Developed for IMSA's "light" class, the GTP was developed by Fiero's design staff, directed by John Schinella. The body was produced in Britain by Spice Engineering of Northamptonshire. It is powered by a Super-Duty engine similar to those that took Fieros to IMSA GTU class wins during the 1985 season. This four-cylinder powerplant produces 330 hp at 7500 rpm. The curb weight of the completed vehicle is only 1,650 lbs.

1986 Expo Commemorative Edition Grand Am

The big event in Canada in 1986--other than the outbreak of a minor trade war with the U.S.--was the Canadian World Exposition in Vancouver, British Columbia. GM Canada built two commemorative vehicles for the Expo, a Chevrolet Astro van and a Pontiac Grand Am. Available in either coupe or sedan form, the Grand Am was silver with blue wheel covers and exterior trim and sported Expo '86 emblems in various places around the car. Some 2,000 were reportedly built in the B-O-C plant in Lansing, Michigan. Other GM commemorative editions were rumored, but the Grand Am and Astro verions were the only two publicized actively by GM.

...And Others

In preparing this book, we researched a wide variety of sources and archives so as to provide the most comprehensive survey of Pontiac show cars, experimentals and special editions. It is certain that we have missed some (although hopefully not many) and we were frustrated to come across information for several for which photos were not available at press time.

1941 Alligator Car

Pontiac built at least one alligator-type show car for the 1941 auto show circuit. The big news in 1941 was the availability in any body style of either a six or an eight cylinder engine for only a modest price differential. Perhaps this car was designed to highlight this news. In any event, the body of the car was sliced in half at the back of the front seat and then hinged at the roof so as to swing upward to reveal the front half of the chassis.

1959 Catalina Pickup

Ford pioneered the car-bodied pickup truck in the United States in 1957 with the Ranchero. Chevrolet was two years behind with their equivalent El Camino. Pontiac built at least one version of the car-bodied pickup in 1959. It shared the roofline styling with the Chevy, but featured the distinctive Pontiac sheetmetal below the beltline. It also featured the Pontiac Wide-Track chassis and drivetrain. The car was painted white and featured Catalina style trim and "spinner" hubcaps. It is currently being restored by a collector in the Midwest.

1968 GTO Hatchback

The hatchback was just beginning to catch on in the late-sixties. Herb Adams built a white GTO hatchback with blue racing stripes in 1968. Hardly anything else is known about it and no photos are known to exist.

Mid-Engined Firebird

Herb Adams also built a mid-engined Firebird in the mid-seventies. Not much else is known about this car an no photos are known to exist.

1969 Firebird Show Car

There was a 1969 Firebird color-and-trim car send around to the auto shows. It was painted yellow and featured yellow mag wheels, then a novelty.

1972 Ventura SD

The Ventura SD was a limited edition Ventura four-door sedan offered only in 1972. About 500 cars were built, primarily for California consumption. Pontiac's West Coast marketing people noticed the European manufacturers were selling increasing numbers of four-door sedans with bucket seats and floor-mounted transmission levers. Pontiac's idea was to offer their smallest sedan (the Ventura) with the bucket seats previously offered only in the coupe. All the parts were there; it was just a matter of arranging them differently. Even the SD identification on the roof sail panel was already in the parts department. It was borrowed from Canada where a number of different SD Acadians and Beaumonts had been offered. "Motor Trend" tested a 1972 Ventura SD equipped with radial tires and a sunroof, but these were not factory options. They were aftermarket items put on the car later. Although the test car had a number of factory options including the 350 cubic inch V-8 engine and Rally Wheels, these were not part of the package. The package included only the bucket seats, carpeting and identification. The rest was left to the buyer's discretion. This project was superceded in 1973 by the new Grand Am four-door sedan which took this concept much farther.

1972 Casa Blanca Grand Ville

The Casa Blanca (white house) was the only show car ever based on the Grand Ville series. Pontiac introduced the Grand Ville with other models for 1971. This was the closest Pontiac ever came to producing a C-body car in the post-war years. The Grand Ville was one of the largest Pontiacs ever built and was positioned just above the Bonneville in the model hierarchy. It shared the same basic B-body as the Bonneville, but used unique formal rooflines on the closed cars that were very similar to those of the C-body Olds 98 and Buick Electra. The Casa Blanca was prepared for the auto show circuit to highlight the Grand Ville series. Being true to its name, everything about this Grand Ville hardtop was white. The exterior and interior were all white, even down to the carpeting on the floor.

Plus...

There are rumors of still other special Pontiacs that were produced over the years. There is, for example, mounting evidence that regional special editions were produced by the Kansas City assembly plant in 1959-1960. Also, a Pontiac Catalina "CXL" model was known to have been sold by Chicago dealers in the 1969-1970 period. Other assembly plants and dealer groups have done similar good deeds from time to time that have gone unrecorded. If we get definitive wind of them, we will try to work them into future editions of this book. We have NOT, however, attempted to list all the aftermarket conversions produced on Pontiac chassis through the years. That would (and may) require another book.

Muscle Pontiacs I and Muscle Pontiacs II contain information not found anywhere else. Volume I includes heavy Trans Am and Fiero coverage and Volume II has much on the Judge, GT-37, E.T. and show cars. From the staff at Bookman Publishing, each is softbound, 96 pages, 8 1/2x11, $8.95.

The GTO Databook & Price Guide includes all the essential data and price information in a handy, pocket-sized format. The current pricing section is of special value to collectors and vendors alike. A tremendous value for $9.95. Softbound, 128 pages, 4 1/2x7.

The Firebird and Trans Am have been an important influence. These books are a detailed inside-and-out examination of the Firebird and Trans Am from the very first one in 1967 right up to 1981. Every production car built in those years is covered in detail using as source material rare, original factory literature. Each is softbound, 144 pages, 7x10, $12.95.

GTO Volume I is one of the most concise histories of the legend. Includes Tri-Powers, Wangers and an extensive section on basic Goat accessories and options. Covers 1964 to 1974. GTO Volume II covers aftermarket literature and manufacturers' information not included in the first volume. New material on Grand Am, 1973 to 1985. Each is softbound, 144 pages, 7x10, $12.95.

The ID Guide contains comprehensive pictorial and statistical coverage of all production models from 1926 to 1966. Every model is shown along essential specs and history. Softbound, 96 pages, 8 1/2x11, $8.95.

Factory literature highlights 15 years of the big machines. Big Pontiacs covers specs and options for all high performance, full-sized Pontiacs from 1955 to 1970, including Bonneville, Catalina, 2+2 and rare Super-Duty engine material. Softbound, 144 pages, 7x10, $12.95.

In celebration of Pontiac's 60th anniversary, this updated version covers every Pontiac produced in the United States, Canada, Australia and other countries. From the original Chief of the Sixes to the Fiero, this 352-page publication is highlighted by hundreds of photos, 26 pages in full color and superior printing. Hardbound, 8 1/2x11, $29.95.

**All books are available through Bookman Publishing
P. O. Box 13492
Baltimore, MD 21203**